Puppy
PARENTING

Puppy PARENTING

WHAT to do and WHEN to do it

Dr Scott Miller

First published in Great Britain in
2007 by Hamlyn
This revised edition published in
2022 by Cassell, an imprint of
Octopus Publishing Group Ltd
Carmelite House
50 Victoria Embankment
London EC4Y 0DZ
www.octopusbooks.co.uk
An Hachette UK Company
www.hachette.co.uk

Distributed in the US by
Hachette Book Group
1290 Avenue of the Americas
4th and 5th Floors
New York, NY 10104

Distributed in Canada by
Canadian Manda Group
664 Annette St.
Toronto, Ontario, Canada M6S 2C8

ISBN 978-1-78840-376-4

A CIP catalogue record for this book
is available from the British Library.

Printed and bound in the United
Kingdom

10 9 8 7 6 5 4 3 2 1

This FSC® label means that materials
used for the product have been
responsibly sourced

Publisher: Trevor Davies
Senior Editor: Faye Robson
Art Director: Jaz Bahra
Designer: Jeremy Tilston
Production Assistant: Serena Savini

Contents

Publisher's note

This is a fully revised edition of the original illustrated book *Puppy Parenting*, published under the imprint Hamlyn in 2007 (ISBN 978-0-60061-426-5).

The advice in this book is provided as general information only. It is not necessarily specific to any individual case and is not a substitute for the guidance and advice provided by a licensed veterinary practitioner consulted in any particular situation. Octopus Publishing Group accepts no liability or responsibility for any consequences resulting from the use of or reliance upon the information contained herein. No dogs or puppies were harmed in the making of this book.

To Summer, Quinn, Jackson, Riley, Zed, Betty, Ricketts, Dave, Skully and Luna – all my babies, both fur and otherwise.

Introduction

Parenting is hard: fact. Parents make mistakes: fact. Parents who make mistakes can still produce healthy, well-balanced adults: fact. Puppy parents are no different and need to cut themselves some slack: fact. The process of puppy parenting should be fun: fact.

With the three pillars of parenting – patience, kindness and consistency – you will be able to parent a puppy into the dog of your dreams, accepting that you will make mistakes along the way. Mistakes are simply a lesson not yet learned, and both you and your puppy are destined to make many as you embark on this exciting but, at points, frustrating journey together. Just remember one thing: your puppy is a dog and not a human; so, if you wish to get it right, you'll naturally need a different parenting style and knowledge base for parenting a puppy from the one you would for parenting kids.

Don't feel the need to sit down and read this book like homework; having a puppy is supposed to be enjoyable and this is not a test.

Puppy Parenting is a manual, a helpful tool (hopefully) and something to dip in and out of for a little guidance as you focus all of your love, attention and time on your wonderful new ball of fluff.

I initially wrote this book after embarking on my own puppy-parenting journey with my, now dearly departed, dog Betty. After a few barren years without a dog in my life, Betty burst onto the scene, bringing carnage, exuberance and, most of all, joy. Watching her grow was a delight and has taught me so much about being a vet and a dog owner.

Since then, and with four human children following Betty's furry footsteps, Skully (aka Skullcrusher…more on that later) joined the family as a tiny white fluffball, capturing the hearts of the entire Miller brood. The lessons learned during the rewarding and, at times, testing journey through puppyhood, and through my job as a vet with 25 years' clinical experience working with puppies and dogs, have inspired me to write this book. I hope that it will enlighten, not dictate, and encourage rather than daunt, by offering simple, practical advice and a month-by-month guide to what you should expect as your puppy grows.

At intervals throughout the book, the guidance it offers is complemented by entries from Betty's and Skully's diaries that provide illuminating episodes from my personal experience. They prove that all of us (even a vet!) can make mistakes, but that we can all learn from these, building our patience and understanding to become good puppy parents. You'll also find answers to all the questions often asked about bringing up a puppy, as well as explanations of 'old wives' tails' – the stories about dogs that are sometimes far from the truth.

Perfect puppy partner

With more than 12 million dogs owned in the UK and more than 90 million in the USA, canine companions are as popular as ever. With the global pandemic, many wannabe dog owners have decided that the time is right to invite a pooch into their lives, leading to a huge rise in the population of dogs across the world. From the microscopic Chihuahua to the giant schnauzer, dogs come in many shapes and sizes to suit their different owners. Short coat or long, affectionate or self-reliant, apartment dwellers or farm animals, dogs have been bred into such varying forms that they can match almost any individual owner's requirements. Rescue dogs have also increasingly become a welcomed and valid choice for many potential pet parents, with canines from countries all over the world needing a fresh start and chance at a loving forever home.

But why do we feel the need to have a dog in the first place? Dogs make noise, take up valuable relaxation time, shed fur and, of course, eat you out of house and home. The answer is simple: because they give us unconditional love. Dogs provide us with a topic of conversation, a reason to venture out of the house and an abundance of joy. They also afford us companionship and protection, and strengthen the family unit by providing a source of humour, a common interest and an outlet for our affection.

It is well documented that the presence of a dog in both home and office environments decreases stress and improves the outlook of those suffering from depression. Canine companions also help foster personal responsibility and understanding of animals in children, as well as encouraging us all to exercise and teaching us how to share. From puppyhood and throughout their lives, dogs maintain a childlike quality that brings out the nurturing side in their human friends, ensuring that our affection for them never diminishes.

Any parent will tell you that to be forewarned is to be forearmed, and puppy parenting is no different. Few events will change your life more dramatically than owning a dog. The advice in this book will fully prepare you for your new parental role, ensuring that your puppy grows into a well-adjusted, healthy and loyal canine companion, who will shower you with love to last a lifetime.

Dr Scott

The potential puppy parent

Dog ownership requires a great deal of consideration – the impulse purchase of a little ball of fur can end in disaster for both you and them. Your environment, bank balance, personality, human and animal housemates, and how much spare time you have are all crucial elements to take into account. This chapter will steer you towards making the right choice of puppy, ensuring a match made in heaven.

Should I own a dog?

Consider carefully

Puppies are undeniably enchanting, though however wonderful they are they remain a huge undertaking and the decision to own one should not be entered into lightly. As a potential future life partner, a canine should not be a fashionable or spur-of-the-moment purchase and many factors must be addressed before a dog is brought into your home. If picking up faeces, clearing up dog hair, having your shoes chewed and going out for walks in all weathers doesn't appeal, then you need not apply for the job of dog owner. But if you have taken all the onerous duties into account and made the decision wisely, choosing to share your life with a dog can lead to one of the most beneficial, enduring and loving relationships that a human being can experience.

Pros

- 🐾 Unconditional love
- 🐾 Companionship
- 🐾 Improved general physical health
- 🐾 Fostering of responsibility in children
- 🐾 Increased interest in the outdoors
- 🐾 Opportunity to meet other dog owners
- 🐾 Decreased stress levels and help in coping with depression

Cons

- 🐾 Responsibility
- 🐾 Cost
- 🐾 Time

What sort of dog is right for me?

Assess your situation

Dogs live for 12 years on average, so the onus is on you as the potential owner to carefully consider your personal circumstances in relation to all the aspects of care that different breeds or types of dog require before choosing and purchasing or re-homing a canine. The key aspects that you need to assess are your living environment, your energy levels and the amount of time and money that you have available to spend on a dog.

Suiting your circumstances

Your environment

Consider the amount of space you have and relate that to the size of dog. For instance, a one-bedroom flat is an inadequate abode for an Irish wolfhound and a country house with plenty of land may be wasted on a Maltese terrier.

Your energy level

This is unlikely to change significantly just because you have a new canine companion, so be honest about how active you are and choose accordingly. A Border collie is highly energetic and intelligent, so purchasing one to keep you company while you watch television will end in tears. Conversely, if you want to spend lots of time enjoying the great outdoors, a shih-tzu will be likely to leave you to do so on your own.

Your cash flow

There can be no doubt that owning a dog is expensive, as they require ongoing nutrition and veterinary treatment at the very bare minimum.

Larger dogs are sure to cost more in food bills alone, so factor this into your decision.

Your time

Some breeds are less time-consuming in terms of grooming or exercise requirements. But any dog will take up, on average, two to three hours per day of your time, and can be left alone for four hours at the very most. Any pet requires care and attention, so if you don't have the time, don't get one.

POTENTIAL OWNER
RÉSUMÉ

Name: A N Owner

Age Adult enough to appreciate the lifelong commitment entered into when getting a dog.

Sex Either sex will enjoy the companionship that a dog can bring.

Height and weight These factors need play little part in which puppy you choose, as long as it is well trained.

Marital and family status The more the merrier. A puppy is a big undertaking for a single owner on a fixed working schedule; partners and children help to share the burden and the rewards.

Nationality All nations of the world are home to dogs and dog owners.

Education A basic appreciation of general care and dog behaviour is all that is needed; much of the learning about a puppy's upbringing is completed 'on the job'.

Occupation Any that allows adequate time to be spent with your new puppy without long periods when they are left on their own.

Activity level Whatever it is currently will increase once a dog is invited into your home.

Personality traits Patient, responsible, trustworthy, loving, hard-working, dedicated, understanding and kind.

Medical complaints Some dogs may have a characteristic that exacerbates a particular condition; excessive moulting, for example, could worsen symptoms of asthma. However, dogs can also help their owners deal with certain complaints. For example, having a dog can aid recovery from illness and combat feelings of loneliness and isolation.

Other interests If you enjoy maintaining a healthy lifestyle and outdoor pursuits such as walking and exploring the countryside, having a well-behaved canine at your side will only increase your pleasure.

POTENTIAL PUPPY
RÉSUMÉ

Name: K-9

Age Eight weeks. Can live up to eighteen years, the average being twelve to fourteen years.

Sex Males and females may vary in size and temperament.

Height and weight Height varies from 7–102cm (3–40in); weight varies from 1–100kg (2–220lb).

Marital and family status Single and looking for love and companionship.

Nationality Originally from the Northern hemisphere, presumably the Middle East, there are hundreds of dog breeds in existence from many nations.

Education Up to you – open to suggestions.

Occupation Potential for skill in hunting, protection, sports and specialist fields (examples of the latter include sniffer, hearing and guide dogs).

Activity level High as a puppy, then can be estimated according to the average activity level of the breed.

Personality traits Loyal, affectionate and honest. Other personality strengths can come from the parents and breed.

Medical complaints From none to many, depending on the individual and breed-specific illnesses.

Other interests Anything that interests you!

BETTY'S DIARY
Visions of you

I had contemplated getting another dog for a long time, but was only just beginning to feel ready after having lost my previous dog, a rescue English bull terrier called Zed, two years earlier. Although Zed had suffered at the hands of his former, neglectful owners, he regained full health to become one of the sweetest and kindest-natured dogs imaginable. Good with other dogs and children, he did his much-maligned breed proud, and when he died my whole family and I were deeply saddened.

I found it difficult to contemplate another dog being more special than my Zed, but eventually came round to the possibility of bringing another canine into my home. For the first time in my life I decided on a puppy, as opposed to re-homing a more mature rescue pet as I had done in the past. I also decided to get a female dog, just to complete the contrast with Zed. As I was living in inner-city London and my outside space was limited to a decent-sized terrace, I decided to choose a smaller dog. I also thought it would be a good idea to get one with short hair, as dog grooming is not my strong suit.

As a vet, I am exposed to the wonderful array of dog breeds brought into the clinic, caring for them at their worst during times of stress, fear or pain. I had always found Border terriers exemplary patients, accepting treatment and afterwards giving a lick on the face as a thank you. They are relatively energetic dogs but also enjoy lazing around the house – a mixture that seemed perfect for me at the time. I am quite an active guy so I liked the idea that a trained terrier would be sociable with all types of people and dogs, would enjoy runs and be entertaining in the park. Although very busy with my work, I rationalized that I would be able to take my new charge to the clinic and the television studio and spend long periods at home with her, so I had the necessary time to dedicate to a canine companion. I was also in a financial position to support a dog, and my job meant minimal vet bills! And so my search for a female Border terrier puppy began...

Should I choose a pure breed or crossbreed?

Do your research

If you are considering a pure-bred dog, you have hopefully chosen based on the breed's suitability to your home and lifestyle. To ensure a pup match made in heaven, you will also then have some guidance on the physical and behavioural requirements and characteristics of that particular breed before they arrive. With development of the many specific breeds of canines now available, pedigree dogs are known to suffer more than crossbreeds from inherited diseases due to inbreeding in order to make them look a certain way (see page 23). Research the different breeds and thoroughly question breeders before choosing a puppy, always asking to meet the parents to assess their temperament, health and surroundings before agreeing to take a pup home.

Crossbreeds have become more commonplace in the last decade, with the rise of the designer breeds such as the cockapoo and labradoodle, and the acceptance that 'rescue' is a new and valid breed to consider. Whether as companions, working dogs or competitors in dog sports, crossbreeds are as adaptable and accessible as pure-bred dogs, and they have fewer inherited health problems. In many cases, meeting the parents of such puppies can be more difficult, as will be determining the potential size and temperament of the pooch when fully grown. Rescue centres are filled with wonderful welfare warriors who go above and beyond to cleverly match rescue dogs to appropriate owners, to ensure that these unfortunate pooches' next move is to their forever home.

SKULLY'S DIARY

Skully was one of six pups born via Caesarean section. Mum Bella (a cross Coton de Tulear and toy poodle) and dad (the very handsome Bichon Frise next door) had come together by chance, with the owners excited to welcome puppies into their loving family home. I was keeping a close eye on developments and supporting the owners, who were a little overwhelmed by the process. Early one afternoon, Bella started to show signs of giving birth. I popped by to support the family as the pups were born, but the more fraught side of having puppies became apparent as Bella struggled for many hours to give birth naturally. We used medication to stimulate contractions and supplement calcium levels, plus some physical techniques to encourage labour, but this failed to help and an ultrasound showed the puppies were becoming distressed. Sadly I therefore made the call to transport her to the vet practice and physically remove them via Caesarean section. Around 2am, with my dedicated team of nurses (who had got out of bed to help) by my side, we managed to save both the exhausted mum and all six puppies, hearing their beautiful squeals as they were revived by the team. On the recovery of Bella and her puppies, their owners were so grateful for our support they very kindly offered me the opportunity to have one of the litter. Amazingly, my wife was at that moment desperate for a little fluffy white dog after years growing up with a West Highland white terrier, and was overjoyed at the chance of having a dog to call her own... The kids, however, had different ideas.

Male vs female?

Take your pick

There is little variability between the sexes to be observed in smaller dogs, but in bigger dogs the differences are more obvious. Male dogs can be more confident and outgoing, but they can also be more aggressive to other dogs. Bitches (actual scientific term) are generally more agreeable in temperament, although this can fluctuate during times of season (averaging twice a year) if they are not spayed. For the purposes of choosing a pet, experience as a vet has proved to me that gender is not a decisive issue. When dogs are neutered (see page 158), there is little difference between the sexes and both make equally wonderful companions.

Which breed should I choose?

Match your personality

Today's dogs come in all shapes and sizes, with more than 200 breeds recognized throughout the world. Pure-bred dogs are categorized in seven main groupings: gundog, hound, pastoral, toy, terrier, utility and working. Then, of course, there is the ever-present and lovable crossbreed, which may also be given the names mongrel, mixed breed, mutt and bitsa (Australian term, as in bits of this and bits of that!) These dogs all belong to the same species, *Canis familiaris*, which means that any two breeds can inter-mate and produce fertile offspring – even in the case of an unlikely pairing between a Great Dane and a Chihuahua! Whatever the breed or breed combination, it will impact on your puppy's physical and behavioural characteristics as an adult, and many owners now consider genetic testing in the pursuit of knowledge about their mixed-breed dog's lineage.

The breed groups are defined mainly by temperament and range from the intelligent and sociable gundogs, who often make great family pets, to the physically imposing working dogs, who need a strong hand and lots of space. Choosing a breed of dog could start with selecting a group that best matches your personality and lifestyle, then narrowing down your choice from there. Breed groupings vary slightly between countries, but the common characteristics for each group are presented on the following pages.

The breed groups

Gundog

Bred to flush and retrieve game, this sporting group, traditionally popular with the shooting fraternity, represents many of the pet canines found in the households of today. Generally medium- to large-sized dogs, the puppies are often highly intelligent and sociable, resulting in an easily trained, affable pet. The oral dexterity demanded by these dogs' historic profession can equate to insatiable chewing in their modern stay-at-home counterparts. The problem can be overcome by supplying them with an interesting array of toys, for which they have a near obsession.

Their boundless capacity for exercise and play is overtaken only by their love of food, so a balance between the two is needed to ensure a healthy and trim dog. These fun-loving and friendly canines enjoy a close bond with their owners and are great pets for children and adults alike. Generally easy to look after, gundogs enjoy nothing more than a long walk and plenty of affection.

Most popular members include: labrador, golden retriever, cocker spaniel, English springer spaniel, Weimaraner and Irish setter.

Hound

Also hunting dogs, hounds would run to catch and hold prey, such as badgers, hares or deer, until their owners arrived on foot or horseback. This behaviour can be translated into non-hunting environments, meaning these canines may chase wildlife in the park or small animals, including cats, at home.

Occasional disobedience and strong will are only minor drawbacks to these highly sociable and friendly dogs. Members of this group are known for their gentle affection towards children and amicable nature when meeting other dogs. Ideal for an active family who enjoy energetic daily walks, they also happily relax at home. Sedentary, overweight hounds may suffer spinal problems as a result of the strain that excess weight puts on their elongated backs.

Most popular members include: dachshund, beagle, whippet, basset hound, greyhound and Afghan hound.

Pastoral

Somewhat ambiguously named, the pastoral group (classified as the herding group in the USA) consists of dogs that are bred to work with domesticated mammals that graze on pastures. These are divided into two subgroupings: herding dogs, which round up flocks of sheep, herds of cattle or even reindeer under the direction of their owners; and protecting dogs, which were bred to live with and look after flocks of sheep.

Herding

Dogs in this subgroup are renowned for their agility, activity and intellect. They are easily trained, reliable and obedient. Many suffer with behavioural problems if not adequately stimulated and require a large amount of exercise if kept in a suburban environment. They have ultra-keen senses, so can be prone to noise phobia or general nervousness unless exposed to traffic and plenty of people as puppies. Their personality traits make them particularly suitable for use in professions such as the police service and they also make excellent candidates for agility competitions.

Most popular members include: corgi, Border collie, bearded collie, German shepherd dog (Alsatian) and Old English sheepdog.

Protecting

The dogs in this pastoral subgroup are known to patrol the house and guard the family. These animals are larger and more powerfully built to enable them to fight off predators and they can be prone to aggression with other dogs and people if they are not adequately socialized. They have also developed a heavier coat to withstand the cold temperatures to which they were traditionally exposed while watching over the sheep or reindeer at night. They tend to be a little stronger-willed, and can be quite stubborn and less energetic than their herding cousins.

Most popular members include: Samoyed, Bergamasco, Komondor and Pyrenean mountain dog.

Toy

These are breeds without any specific active purpose, and are regarded as companions. Usually small in stature, they are easily trained and very agreeable, enjoying play and entertaining their owners. Since they are small dogs, they can be frightened of children and other dogs. They are also easy to spoil and thus are prone to obesity. Not being particularly active dogs, these canines are disinclined to take long walks, preferring lots of fuss and attention from their devoted owners.

Most popular members include: Chihuahua, cavalier King Charles spaniel, Bichon Frise and pug.

Terrier

Known for their energetic and independent nature, terriers were originally bred to catch and kill small mammals considered to be vermin. Foxes, badgers, rats and rabbits would fall victim to these tenacious and feisty canines, which carry the instinct to hunt and kill into the home environment. Given that they like to give chase and bite hard, terriers can pose a threat to cats and other small mammals if they do not have exposure to them as puppies. Yet terriers remain one of the most popular groups of canine pet, with strong protective instincts, energetic personalities and the ability to entertain themselves at home with toys.

A good daily walk is all that is needed for most terriers as long as they are supplied with games and suitable toys, with which they will run around the house. Tending to be a vocal group of dogs, terriers can be regarded as either good watchdogs or rather noisy, depending on the circumstances, and are variable in their behaviour towards other dogs.

Most popular members include: Jack Russell terrier, fox terrier, West Highland white terrier, Staffordshire bull terrier and bull terrier.

Utility

Otherwise known as the non-sporting group, this category encompasses a mixture of dogs that have been bred to undertake a variety of tasks, generally other than hunting, within human society. Consequently these breeds come in all manner of shapes, coats and sizes. They excel in herding and guarding, and many individuals within the group have shown exceptional bravery and valour in their protective roles towards humans. As utility dogs vary greatly in temperament, owners usually choose a type on the basis of appearance and then research each breed's specific traits.

Most popular members include: shih-tzu, bulldog, Dalmatian, poodle and schnauzer.

Working

Usually bred as guard dogs, these are large to extra-large dogs with great physical presence. They are also used in specialized search-and-rescue fields. Requiring moderate exercise and plenty of food, these big dogs need a lot of space and a big budget. They are very loyal to their owners, but strict leadership is needed from the outset of buying a puppy to ensure that you are fully in control of these strong beasts into adulthood. These giants of the dog world tend to be the shortest-lived of all breed groups.

Although generally having shorter fur and therefore minimal grooming requirements, working dogs demand more specialist care and ownership than other breeds. A big responsibility in more ways than one, working breeds are not recommended for the first-time dog owner.

Most popular members include: boxer, doberman, rottweiler, Great Dane, St Bernard and bullmastiff.

Crossbreeds

Many dogs are a combination of two of more breeds, resulting in offspring that can vary greatly in size, appearance and personality. As a result of mixed parentage, these dogs tend to avoid many of the inherited diseases seen in pure-bred dogs.

With much greater variability within the gene pool, a crossbred puppy can undergo significant change as it develops, to grow into a dog on a scale that you hadn't expected. The temperament and strength of crossbreeds are also variable. Given responsible ownership and love, these dogs can make just as good companions as their shorter-lived, pure-bred counterparts.

If a crossbred puppy is acquired from a local welfare centre or dog home, you are doubling your achievement, as you are giving a home to a puppy that desperately needs one at the same time as gaining a new life partner.

Most popular types include: labradoodle, cockapoo, puggle and mongrel (no definable type or breed).

How do I find a puppy?

Select your source

Once you have identified a breed of dog that fits your personality and lifestyle, the next step is to find a litter of puppies. There are many ways to source a breeder or welfare centre: via the internet, library, newspapers, magazines or word of mouth. Dog shows also offer the opportunity to learn more about your chosen breed, obtain contact details of local breeders and find out when puppies may be due. Many countries worldwide have their own national Kennel Club – a respected organization that offers an ideal starting point for gaining information about breeders and dog breeds alike.

Always Google-search breeders and look for any negative reviews, as unscrupulous breeders or third-party sellers abound, fuelling the trade of puppy farms to the detriment of animal welfare. A good technique for this is searching the phone number given by the breeder online, as this can unmask breeders who have multiple websites with different breeds of dogs, which would pose a big red flag. Do this work BEFORE going anywhere near a seller, as once you clap your eyes on an adorable puppy, whether healthy or not, you may, like many dog lovers, find it almost impossible to resist taking them home.

Be prepared

It is always a good idea to have a basic knowledge of dogs and your specific breed before you begin searching for puppies. This information will help you to distinguish between respectable breeders or welfare centres and pretenders.

Be discerning

If you find the breeders or vendors to be unfriendly, unhelpful or not particularly knowledgeable, take your leave. Honest breeders will openly discuss the negative attributes of their breed along with the positive ones, as they will want their puppies to go to suitable homes and not just anyone with the right purchase price in their pocket.

Much of a puppy's behaviour comes from their parents and socialization with humans in the early stages of life. If something doesn't feel right or you don't quite gel with the breeder or parents, it's possible that some of that less-than-desirable personality may rub off on the puppy. If you are at all concerned regarding a breeder's credibility, it is best to take your custom elsewhere. In any case, it is advisable not to buy a puppy on first viewing, but to allow yourself the necessary time and space to consider the purchase without feeling pressured.

Look for cleanliness

General hygiene should always be highly regarded. Puppies who have been living in squalid conditions and who have been exposed to disease are more likely to suffer from a weakened immune system into adulthood. Before you even consider buying a puppy, check out the cleanliness of the establishment. If it doesn't match your high expectations, or you are not given the opportunity to visit the birthplace of the litter in question, either in person or at least via video, you should take your search for a healthy puppy elsewhere.

What to ask the breeder

About the parents

Always ask to meet the parents of puppies so that you are aware of the size of dog that your puppy will eventually become. The personality of your puppy can also be gauged by their parents, so if both parents are friendly and easy-going, then you can assume that their puppies will have a similar temperament. If the breeder is unable to show you the parents, be very dubious of the sale. Beware of puppy farms, where females are constantly bred without their health and wellbeing taken into account, producing as many puppies as possible for the pet trade. Parent dogs kept in such circumstances will be thin and in poor condition generally, so are likely to be kept away from prospective new owners. It is now illegal in the UK to sell puppies that are not kept with their parents, so be careful to avoid third-party sellers who buy dogs from multiple litters to sell for a profit with no regard for their welfare.

About microchipping, vaccinations and worming

Always ask about the details of the puppy's vaccination and worming history and make sure you obtain written evidence from the breeder, signed by a vet. All puppies in the UK must be microchipped by law, should have been vaccinated once prior to sale and have had at least one worming treatment as a bare minimum. If any of this has not been done, again be dubious of the sale and don't commit.

About illnesses and inherited diseases

Ask if there are any known illnesses in the puppy's family or breed. If your choice of breed is known to be at risk from suffering inherited disease (see opposite), discuss this from the outset with the breeder and ask to see reports confirming the puppy's parents' genetic health. This could include

X-ray reports of hip scoring and DNA, eye tests or blood-test results, which should confirm that the parents of your puppy are fit to breed.

PAWS FOR THOUGHT
Inherited diseases

Pure-bred dogs by definition have required some inbreeding during the development of the breed in order to attain a particular set of characteristics. With intensive breeding, physical traits such as coat appearance and body structure have been fine-tuned and passed on to offspring via genetic information stored in DNA. The concentration of these positive traits has also accumulated inherited diseases, passed on genetically from parent to offspring. Commonly noted inherited defects include heart murmurs in cavalier King Charles spaniels, degenerative joint disease in German shepherd dogs, eye problems and BOAS (brachycephalic obstructive airway syndrome) in French bulldogs and skin disease in Shar Peis.

Respectable breeders do their utmost to ensure that puppies produced by them shed the negative genetic attributes of their breed by mating only those dogs free of inherited conditions. Some breeds are becoming increasingly unhealthy as a result of extreme breed standards, leading to lifelong ill health and discomfort, and causing great concern among veterinarians around the world. Be aware of any known genetic disorders carried by your breed of choice, and discuss these fully with your vet and breeder before purchasing a new puppy. Finding out about these conditions will help you to choose a healthy puppy and avoid inheriting your own set of problems, both financial and emotional.

What if I have a cat?

Consider your feline's personality

Think carefully about the personality of your cat before contemplating a dog, as a cat of a nervous disposition may totally reject the idea of a canine companion, choosing to vacate your house or injure the new arrival. In any event, there will be troubled times ahead, with extra work and attention needing to be given to both animals to help ease the situation. Most cats will not appreciate the new smells and sounds or the unwanted attentions of the puppy and may lash out aggressively or hide away in the early stages of introduction. Generally cats are as adaptable as dogs and will find their way to make peace with the situation; just make sure that they can escape your playful puppy and are offered the same amount of affection that they were afforded pre-pooch.

Avoid inappropriate breeds

Some dog breeds have strong hunting instincts (see pages 16 and 18), so this should be considered when choosing a puppy to enter a home containing a resident feline or other smaller pets.

What if I have another dog?

Counteract jealousy

As dogs are pack animals, most will enjoy the company of another member of their species and will welcome the attention offered by a puppy. It may take a few days for your older dog to come to terms with the new arrival, however, so make sure that you lavish more affection on them than you did before the puppy arrived to avoid jealousy.

Proceed with care

Dogs are aware of the relative age of a puppy and generally modify their responses accordingly, but do not allow yourself to lapse into a false sense of security and expect that your current canine companion will naturally accept your new arrival with ease. You will need to introduce them in a controlled way and oversee their interactions for the first few weeks, using baby gates and crates as an excellent way to keep an exuberant puppy contained and give your resident dog the chance for some peace.

Form an orderly queue

You should have a good idea of how your existing dog behaves with other dogs. When considering a new pooch, your resident dog should be put first, showing them the respect and consideration they deserve by assessing what impact a new puppy will have on them. If, after honest reflection, you conclude that your current dog is stalwartly antisocial in nature, unwell or may find a new arrival too stressful, the acquisition of a puppy may not be an appropriate move and will have to wait.

What if I have children?

Choose an appropriate breed

Most puppies enjoy the company of children, who are generally smaller and less frightening than the much larger adult humans. Certain dog breeds are known for their excellent temperament around children, but other breeds with strong prey instincts may be more unpredictable.

Research the breeds of dog that you are considering in terms of their behaviour around children, asking the breeder for advice regarding this important character trait. If you have very small children in your home, it is paramount that you choose a dog with a genetic predisposition to good behaviour around children and take into consideration the size of the fully grown dog in relation to your growing family. No child should ever be left alone in a room with a dog; it is not fair on either of them. The combination of two sentient beings who at times behave erratically, both physically and emotionally, is not great, and should never be allowed unsupervised, no matter how chilled out the parties concerned are. Always chaperone interactions to ensure safety for all involved and teach children how to behave correctly with their new furry friend.

Child-friendly breeds

Airedale terrier
Cairn terrier
cavalier King Charles spaniel
golden retriever
labrador
Newfoundland
poodle
pug
schnauzer
whippet

Child-Friendly mixed breeds

cockapoo
labradoodle
puggle

How do I choose a puppy?

Make an informed choice

Choosing a well-balanced, healthy puppy is not as easy as it seems. Forearm yourself with some basic knowledge to complement your common sense. Be sensible in your choice – don't let guilt lead you to choose a weak, ill or nervous puppy. A poor health record as a puppy can lead to a weakened immune system and other health issues as an adult, resulting in financial and emotional burdens that may be hard to cope with. Such an individual is best kept in the capable hands of the breeder and their mum. Always reserve the right to say no. In fact, lead with a no, as the overwhelming sense of wanting to say yes to those puppy-dog eyes will consume you...you have been warned!

Temperament indicators

The puppy you choose should be alert and interested in you, without showing overt signs of aggression. The opposite extreme is not a good choice either – a fearful puppy indicates either inherent nervousness or poor socialization of the puppies by the vendor.

What to look for

Pick up the puppy and they should feel heavier than you expect; a light or thin puppy could indicate ill health. The puppy should be relaxed in your grasp and, when released, interact well with you and their littermates, giving an indication of the type of dog they will become. You should also carry out a basic health check (see page 28).

When should I take the puppy home?

Optimum age

Your puppy should be at least eight weeks of age. Any younger and they may be too weak or improperly weaned to be torn away from mum. At eight weeks puppies are at the optimum developmental stage to leave their littermates and begin life in a new home. They have developed enough canine social and play skills by being with their siblings and mother and now need to understand humans and how to relate to their world.

Basic health check

Eyes

These should be bright and fully open, with no discharge or redness, as this can indicate disease.

Gums

These should be pink, indicating that the puppy is healthy and not anaemic from worms or ill health.

Genitals and anus

Males should have two testicles descended; if not, the puppy is classified as cryptorchid and will require surgical treatment to correct the condition. Females should have a clean vulva. Both sexes should be checked for any diarrhoea staining around the anus, which could indicate gut upsets, worms or early digestive problems.

Ears

Check that there is no wax build-up in the ear canals and no smell evident, which could indicate infection. Check the pinnae (ear flaps) for skin disease.

Skin and coat

A shiny coat free of dandruff indicates a healthy dog. Patches of hair loss and scabbing lesions could indicate fungal infection or external parasite infestation.

Umbilicus (belly button)

Check that this is flat; a swelling near this site can indicate hernia and may need surgical correction.

Feet and nails

Dogs have five toes on the front feet and generally four on the back, occasionally with a dewclaw (the functionless remnant of a big toe) on the inside of the hind leg. All nails should be intact and unbroken.

Preparing for parenthood

BEFORE YOUR PUPPY ARRIVES

Once you have chosen your puppy, or even before, you will need to make changes to your home environment and assemble various items of equipment in preparation for the new arrival – yes, it's just like having a baby! This is also a good time to survey the bewildering range of canine feeding options on offer.

Puppy paraphernalia

Think ahead

It is important to consider all the wants and needs of your new puppy before they arrive on your doorstep. From where they will sleep to what they will play with, a lot of equipment is needed to keep your puppy healthy and happy. The following is a rundown of the required basics.

Food and water bowls

Plastic, stainless steel or ceramic, dog bowls come in many shapes and sizes and are a good idea to ensure a hygienic household. Plastic bowls should have a wide rim and stopper pads beneath to avoid sliding, although be mindful that the puppy may chew on more than just the food. It is essential to have at least two bowls, one for food and one for water. Fresh water should be available to your puppy at all times, so put their water bowl in a low-traffic place where it won't be knocked over.

Toys

Puppy toys are an important tool in the war against chewing. They also stimulate your dog's interest in play and in investigating their environment. There is a huge array of puppy toys on the market. Be selective and choose ones that are non-toxic and have no detachable parts or sharp edges. Rubber toys are an excellent choice as they have an appealing texture and are different from other materials in your home that your puppy may wish to chew, such as clothes and furniture.

It is a good idea to have a few different toys on rotation to offer the puppy at various times of the day. This helps to avoid boredom, and also serves to show you which they enjoy best. Regularly check toys for damage and provide new ones to keep your puppy both safe and stimulated.

Crates, playpens and bedding

The easiest way of setting up your puppy's bedroom is using a puppy crate or playpen. Usually of stainless steel construction, these foldable cages are large enough for your puppy both to play and sleep in comfortably. A puppy crate is smaller and includes a roof and a floor, while a playpen simply fences off a larger area. A playpen will allow the puppy to be contained out of harm's way during the day, enabling you to carry out household chores in peace. It will also provide the puppy with a secure sleeping enclosure at night. Place the crate or pen in a room where people frequently pass through, such as the kitchen, to make sure that the puppy does not feel excluded from the activities of the home.

A basic puppy enclosure should contain bedding in the form of blankets or a vet bed (purpose-designed animal bedding used in vet clinics and obtained from most pet retailers), an absorbent puppy training pad, a water bowl and toys. As an extra comfort for your new puppy, it is a good idea to add a blanket that carries mum's scent (see page 66), either laid on top of the bedding or vet bed, or crumpled into a corner for the puppy to nuzzle.

Baskets or boxes

If you decide on giving your puppy the run of the house (you're brave!) then hard plastic, cloth or wicker baskets are available. Bear in mind that your puppy will get bigger, so either choose a basket large enough for an adult specimen of your puppy's breed or use a temporary cardboard box until your puppy has grown. Place the bed somewhere warm and out of draughts, remembering to add a blanket with mum's scent.

Baby gate

This is a very useful purchase to help control an adventurous puppy as they grow. It can prevent accidents in the kitchen and elsewhere, stop the puppy from going out the front door or up the stairs and confine them to certain parts of the home.

Collars

It is worthwhile investing in a collar and lead from day one to get your puppy acclimatized to them. Wearing a collar early prepares your puppy for the big outside world that awaits when their vaccination course has been completed. In many countries, such as the UK and Australia, it is law for dogs to wear a collar and ID tag when out and about, so it's important to get your puppy used to comfortably wearing them as a normal part of life. A specially designed and engraved identity tag to place on your puppy's collar, with your contact details in case they go missing, is a great first piece of puppy bling!

Available in a wide variety of colours, a collar should be chosen for its suitability for your puppy and not its appearance. A collar should be lightweight, with no sharp edges, and loose enough to place at least two fingers between the collar and your puppy's neck. Check the fit before securing it around your puppy's neck and use for short but increasing periods each day. Remember to loosen the collar as your puppy grows.

Harnesses

Chiefly made of strong nylon, harnesses avoid pressure around the neck and can be used along with a collar if your dog is strong, to help better keep them under control. Choke chains are antiquated and aversive, potentially life threatening and should not be used. Such archaic methods of control are in any case unnecessary if you are patient and a consistent training regime is implemented early on.

Leads

These are available in rope, leather, chain, nylon or a mixture of materials. It is useful to have both a short and a long lead to keep your puppy in check – the shorter lead is suitable for initial indoor use, while 10-foot (3-metre) or even 15-foot (4.5-meter) leads are ideal when your growing puppy is allowed more freedom to burn off some of that youthful exuberance.

Grooming equipment

You will need a brush or comb to maintain your puppy's appearance, whatever the breed. Each breed has different grooming needs, so ask the breeders what they use to groom their adult dogs. Getting your puppy used to being brushed early on is important if regular visits to the grooming parlour will be required in the future.

Nail clippers are used by many dog owners to avoid scratches from sharp-nailed puppies. However, given that blood vessels and associated nerves are present in your puppy's nails, it is advisable to have a lesson from your vet or groomer before attempting to clip nails at home. Grinders are also available to shorten the nail keratin without cutting, and can prove a safer method for many concerned about the regularly fraught first attempts at nail clipping.

The food you will need

Don't be daunted

Your ravenous puppy needs to eat four times a day and grows on average 12 times faster than a human child, so choosing the right food for them is paramount. Canine diets can be just as complex and varied as human ones, containing varying levels of protein, carbohydrate (sugar), lipid (fat), vitamins and minerals from many different sources. With a multitude of diets available, and making the right choice critical to a puppy's development, many owners find decisions regarding nutrition daunting. With information showered upon you by breeders, vets and other dog owners, the best piece of advice is to keep it simple. Whatever food you choose, always supply your puppy with fresh water.

COMMON QUESTIONS
Feeding

How often and when do I feed my puppy?

Four times daily at evenly spaced intervals is recommended for an eight-week-old puppy, gradually reducing the frequency of meals over time. Fresh water should be constantly available. Always feed your puppy after you have eaten – this is a good way to reinforce the message that they are subordinate to you and your family in the dominance hierarchy. Try to feed your puppy at around the same times every day, remembering that canines thrive off consistency; this will also help you to determine when they will defecate (generally within 20 minutes or so after eating), resulting in easier house-training.

Isn't it boring for a dog to feed them the same food all the time?

No. Dogs tend to eat and enjoy one type of food throughout their lives. If you offer them many different types of food, they will choose the one to eat based on taste, not on whether it is the best for them nutritionally. Also, changes in diet can cause gut upsets, leading to diarrhoea and weight loss. At the young puppy stage, you need to be firm in choosing a good-quality complete balanced food and sticking with it.

Dry versus moist diets

Dry complete foods are generally recommended over moist canned foods by vets, but there are advantages and disadvantages to both.

Dry diets are good for oral health, as they have an abrasive effect on the teeth when eaten. They are also relatively economical and, as they tend to be more concentrated, with less volume than moist foods, produce a smaller amount of faeces. Dry foods also last better when served, though the use of preservatives gives some puppy parents cause for concern.

Dry foods may, however, be less palatable to your dog than the moist varieties, as they have a less pronounced aroma. This can be addressed by using warm water in the early stages to increase scent throw and improve palatability. Moist foods also offer a wider choice. On the other hand, moist foods store poorly once opened and can readily attract flies in hot weather. A moist diet is also not beneficial to your dog's oral health.

Complete diets versus complementary foods and supplements

Complete diets are just that – complete, providing all dietary needs for optimal canine health. When a dog food uses the term 'complete balanced diet', the manufacturer must adhere to strict guidelines in its production, with the resultant diet scientifically balanced with everything nutritionally required by a growing puppy. Complete diets make feeding straightforward, as all premium complete diets are nutritionally balanced. They also contain top-quality ingredients, resulting in a visibly healthy puppy. The downside is that these sorts of foods are relatively expensive, though investing in a high-quality food will lead to a healthier dog that will need less frequent trips to the vet.

Complementary foods (such as treats and chews) are those that have to be combined with other foods to provide for your puppy's nutritional needs. They are usually packaged in a semi-moist form. As they are not completely nutritionally balanced, complementary foods cannot form the sole basis of your dog's diet. Although they add dietary variety, they can also complicate feeding as you must combine carefully selected foodstuffs or supplements to give your puppy all that they require. When you see the term 'complementary' used, you know that it is not a food that can be fed in isolation.

Commercially prepared foods versus home-cooked meals

Commercial dog foods are mass-produced and specifically designed for optimal canine health. They are readily available and easy to use, but lack variability in texture.

Some breeders and owners still advocate and insist upon home-cooked meals. These have the advantages of containing fresh ingredients and offering variety. However, if you are cooking meals for your dog yourself, there is a risk that you won't provide all the necessary vitamins and minerals.

Maintaining the optimum nutritional balance is not easy, especially if you have a growing puppy. A home-cooked diet is also time-consuming to prepare. If you opt for this method, ask your vet for advice and ensure that your puppy is regularly checked to detect any deficiencies before they cause irreparable health damage.

Organic diets

There are also dog foods available that are formulated with raw materials sourced only from high-quality organic farms. These sorts of organic foods should display a label of certification. These are environmentally responsible products that are as nutritionally balanced and of as good quality as their non-organic counterparts, but can carry a higher price tag.

Vegetarian diets

Some dog owners are vegetarian and would like to feed their puppies with a similarly meat-free diet. Although this is a respectable and environmentally sound choice to make for themselves and the planet, it is not recommended for growing puppies. Wild canines enjoy an omnivorous (mixture of meat and vegetable) diet; it is very difficult to correctly balance a vegetarian diet for a growing puppy and failure to do so can easily cause nutrient deficiencies that could result in disease as they mature.

Solely vegetarian diets have been recently developed to provide complete balanced nutrition for adult dogs, using proteins in peas and eggs as alternatives to meat. They may not be the first choice for many dogs and dog owners but do have strong ethical and environmental credentials, so may be worth taking a look at, or using sporadically alongside meat or insect-based foods.

Raw foods

The feeding of raw foods to dogs is currently a popular dietary trend that has come with its share of controversy. A raw-food diet is exactly what it sounds like: your dog is fed ingredients that are not cooked. It contains a mixture of meat, vegetables and fruits, which many pundits feel is more aligned to what dogs would eat in the wild. There are no scientific studies to back up the findings, but proponents of raw-food diets report signs of brighter dogs with shinier coats and reduced frequency and scent of faeces. The downsides are the potential for a greater environmental pawprint in their production and distribution, and the fact that raw foods can be exposed to dangerous bacteria such as *E. coli* and Salmonella during delivery. Bacteria, parasites and other pathogens that are normally killed by the cooking process are a risk to both owners and dogs. Some raw-food diets are not completely balanced and must be supplemented for optimal canine health.

Insect-based diets

An interesting and exciting doggy dietary development, insect-based foods are a new arrival to the pet-food market. They significantly reduce your dog's carbon pawprint, and have good palatability and high-quality protein and hypoallergenic properties, so are a valid option for the environmentally conscious canine owner to consider. An insect-based diet is currently an expensive choice but, as pet food is thought to make up around one quarter of the world's meat consumption, and its production and resultant environmental impacts are well documented, your new-age dog might not turn their nose up at an insect-based diet in future.

Treats

Titbits and treats will invariably be given to your puppy during training, but they must be taken into account when calculating the total amount of energy (calories) consumed each day by your puppy. Excess weight can cause extra stress on joints, lead to strain on the heart and liver, and result in an unhealthy, overweight adult dog.

Choose a treat that is meat-based or cereal-based and specifically designed for dogs. Human foods, such as sweet biscuits or potato crisps, offer little nutritional value to your puppy. It is suggested that more than 40 per cent of the world's dogs are currently clinically obese. Strictly measuring out the food given to your puppy as meals after treats have been factored in is an important start to keeping their weight under control in the long term.

Puppy- and breed-specific diets

You can buy specifically formulated puppy diets. These are not just a marketing ploy and are definitely worth considering because they contain higher nutrient levels to support the rapid rate of early growth in your puppy.

A breed-specific diet is another option that is well worth thinking about. Good-quality breed-specific diets take into account all of your dog's requirements, because manufacturers have studied the breed's particular development patterns to supply the exact nutrients needed to promote optimal growth and health. These diets cater individually for large-, medium- and small-breed dogs, aiming to meet the different and changing nutritional needs of each group as the dogs mature. Most offer a weight or age chart so that you can be sure to feed the right amounts of food as your puppy grows.

Supplements

From essential fatty acids to glucosamine, pre- and postbiotics to curcumin, there is real benefit in looking further than the basics of canine nutrition to help give your dog their best possible life. With more research showing the positive effects of active ingredients that go beyond simply protein, carbohydrates, fats, vitamins and minerals, there is a wealth of supplements on the market that help to support the brain, heart, skin, joint and immune-system health of our pups. Just be sure to research the company and make sure that products are ethically sourced, pure, powerful and proven to help the growing pooch in your life.

COMMON QUESTIONS
Feeding

What happens if my puppy won't eat the food I offer?
Puppies will generally inhale food in an impressive fashion, so if your puppy doesn't eat the food as soon as you place it down, they probably won't eat it at all. Leave it for five minutes only, then pick

it up, cover it and wait an hour or so. This wait will stimulate your puppy's appetite, stop the food going off (which would further put them off it) and avoid teaching them that abstinence will get them something different. If your pup is really stubborn, try mixing their food with some warm water, which will increase its smell and soften it, helping to improve its palatability. Many puppies won't eat particularly well for the first few days in a new home, as there is so much excitement, exploration and playing to be done. If you are worried, weigh them on some home scales daily to assure yourself that they continue to gain healthy weight. Always consult a vet if you are concerned.

Is ordinary chocolate dangerous for dogs to eat?

Chocolate – or, more accurately, the active ingredient theobromine present in cocoa – is toxic to dogs. Eaten in large amounts, theobromine can cause bleeding disorders and severe diarrhoea in canines, which can prove fatal. In addition, grapes or their dried varieties, onions and garlic should not be fed to dogs, since they can also be damaging or fatal for your pup if digested.

OLD WIVES' TAIL

Feeding your dog raw bones will make them become aggressive.

Raw bones (or any raw food, for that matter) will not make your dog aggressive. While cooked bones splinter and can cause constipation and obstruction, raw bones crush when bitten and are much safer for your dog to consume. However, all bones can potentially lodge in your puppy's gut, so it is best to give chews specifically designed to improve your dog's dental health and leave real bones off the puppy menu. Raw meat sourced from a respected butcher is acceptable, but animals can pick up parasites by consuming raw meat that is not of high hygienic quality. It can also be difficult to achieve a good balance of vitamins and minerals in home-prepared meals (see pages 38 and 39), so keeping to complete balanced diets is easier and ultimately better for your dog than feeding them on raw meat.

COMMON QUESTIONS
Feeding

Can I change the food that the breeder was feeding my puppy?

Yes you can, as long as you do it gradually. There may be a few occasions in your puppy's life when you need to alter their diet, so slowly introduce the new food with the old so that the puppy gets used to the difference in size, flavour and/or texture. Sudden changes can result in diarrhoea, so change a diet gradually over a week and be prepared for some softer stools to be produced during that time.

How do I know if I am feeding my puppy the right food in the right amounts?

Regularly assess your puppy, checking that they have bright eyes, a glossy coat, a wet nose and a bright disposition. A puppy should always have a visible 'waist' and ribs that can be felt, indicating that they are not becoming overweight. Arrange regular check-ups with your vet and also weigh your puppy regularly at home to confirm that you have them on the right dietary track.

I have another dog. How will this affect feeding the puppy?

Feed your puppy after your adult dog has finished eating so that there is no possibility of annoyance or food-motivated aggression from the older dog. Pick up any other dogs' or cats' bowls so that the puppy has access only to their own food.

Puppy-proofing your home and garden

Take pre-emptive action

Your new puppy's exploration and investigation of their environment and all that it contains are important and entertaining components of your their development. Since your adventurous puppy will be chewing, licking, pawing and nudging their way through your home, precautions need to be taken to avoid accident or injury to them as well as to safeguard your property.

Think of your puppy's arrival in terms of a visiting human toddler with an amazing sense of smell, sharp teeth and an appetite for destruction. You should assess what would prove inviting to such a child in your home and then move all these attractive, non-puppy items out of reach. By removing or eliminating potential hazards, you will ensure that your new puppy has a happy and relaxed arrival, minimize the risk of accidents and unnecessary vet bills, and avoid the fallout of ruining your and your family's valued belongings.

Establish ground rules

Before your puppy arrives, it is best to lay down some basic ground rules with regard to where they can and can't go. Designate some rooms, such as bedrooms, out of bounds to your puppy to confine the cleaning up. Make sure that everyone in the family knows that these are puppy-free zones and use baby gates or closed doors to enforce the no-go areas. Consequently these rooms won't need to be kept so tidy and the belongings within them will be safe from a chewing puppy. This will also instil in your puppy that they cannot follow you everywhere, which will help to build their confidence in being left alone and be beneficial as they mature and you need to leave the house.

Decide where your puppy will toilet – that is, which spot indoors or outdoors. Many people are concerned that puppy pads may encourage a puppy to always wish to toilet indoors, which in my experience is not the case. If your puppy will be toileting outdoors, will they have the run of the garden or just a small section? Although puppies should be supervised at all times in the early days, you may suddenly and unavoidably need to be elsewhere; defining where would be a safe room or 'den' for your young pup if you have to briefly leave them alone is also worth considering.

Prepare puppy zones

Once you have decided in which rooms your puppy will be allowed to roam freely, set about puppy-proofing them. Here you should be considering both the safety of your puppy and the protection of your property. Keep all poisonous plants or products out of the puppy's potential reach; tidy away dangling electrical wires and toys; and check for gaps that your puppy could get through or get caught under as they explore their new home.

The ways in which the most commonly used areas of the home – kitchen, living room and garden – should be puppy-proofed are described over the following pages.

Kitchen

Rubbish bin

Choose a tall bin with a secure lid to avoid the puppy raiding it.

Floors

Use non-toxic detergents for cleaning. As floors are generally slippery, avoid playing with your puppy on them. Keep your personal belongings off the floor to avoid them being chewed up or urinated on.

Cupboards

Check for gaps beneath that the puppy could squeeze into and consider placing child safety locks on the doors to avoid them accessing the contents.

Appliances

Your puppy may find it a great game to hide in open dishwashers, washing machines and refrigerators, with potentially disastrous consequences, so make sure that they all close firmly. The oven should also be kept closed and you should get in the habit of turning saucepan handles inwards to prevent spillage when your puppy gets taller.

Tea towels

These are perfect for your puppy to chew on, so keep them out of reach.

Food and drink

Don't tempt a puppy to jump up by leaving food lying around on surfaces or low tables. Unsupervised hot drinks can be spilled and lead to injury. Remember to tidy up straight away – and if you think, *Maybe I shouldn't leave that food out*, then don't!

Living room

Televisions, lamps and other electrical equipment
Check for dangling cables and wires that may be fun for your puppy to tug on or chew.

Rugs
During the early days, it is a good idea to roll up and store away any rugs that you value. Rugs are prime candidates for chewing and your new puppy is also highly likely to urinate on them.

Coffee table
If tables are quite low, don't leave food, drinks or papers on them as these are all items that your puppy will be keen to investigate.

Ornaments
Any breakable objects need to be placed up high out of reach of the puppy or stored away to prevent accidents.

Personal belongings
Shoes and slippers may have been left strewn around the living room before the puppy arrived, but this is no longer an option. If you want them kept intact, put them away.

Open fires
A dangerous feature for a puppy, who won't understand that a fire is a no-go zone. Puppy burns and sooty footprints await the owner who doesn't invest in a protective fireguard or partition.

Curtains and blinds

Cords or curtain ties are great fun to play with, so tuck them away before your puppy discovers them.

Garden

Boundary fences

To keep your puppy safe and secure into adulthood, check for broken sections, holes and sharp edges. If you have hedges, look for gaps and fill them with meshing if necessary. The average fence height for containing a larger, agile dog can exceed 2.5m (8ft), while a small terrier would be adequately contained by a 1.2m (4ft) fence. Ask your breeder what height is required to keep an adult dog contained.

Ponds, water features and swimming pools

All are potentially deadly to the adventurous new arrival, so keep your puppy safe by securely fencing off anything like this.

Plants and flowerbeds

Whether they are prickly, poisonous or precious, plants are a constant source of amusement to a puppy. If you want to keep your plants intact and your puppy healthy and safe, fence them off or place pots up high until the dreaded chewing has diminished.

Garden shed

Keep the door to a garden shed or other storage area securely locked, as these places are likely to contain pesticides and other potentially hazardous substances and objects.

Gates

Ensure that any gates to the outside world are secure. Replace locks if necessary and keep the gates safely closed at all times.

Hosepipe

A perfect chewing toy, a hosepipe can be damaged by your puppy or they can get caught up in it. Keeping it wound up and out of reach can prevent mishaps.

The V.E.T.

GETTING THE BEST TREATMENT

The veterinary clinic is an essential part of your new puppy's healthcare, but the mere sound of the word 'vet' can evoke a fearful response in many canine companions. Developing a good relationship with your vet early on will keep visits enjoyable, without resorting to spelling out the dreaded word V. E. T. to keep your puppy calm.

Choosing a good vet

Do some market research

The service provided by veterinary clinics can vary dramatically. Visit the local practices without your puppy, checking services and approachability of staff. Focus on hygiene levels rather than on fees, as your puppy deserves the best treatment in a quality establishment. Ask other dog owners for advice, as most people are keen to speak highly of their vet if the service has been outstanding. Check online forums and reviews, but don't let one bad review stop you visiting to meet the veterinary team for yourself.

Count the cost

It is pertinent to reaffirm here that owning a dog is not cheap and all potential veterinary costs should be considered before you buy one. In the worst-case scenario, your puppy may turn out to be a sickly or accident-prone individual and fees for veterinary treatment will be compounded by the cost of all the preventative medications and food essential for keeping them healthy. Pet insurance is widely available and should help towards the cost of illness or injury, so compare insurers and coverage to make sure you can provide your pup with the best veterinary care available.

When to go and what to expect

Early introductions

To benefit both your puppy's health and behavioural development, it is a good idea to pay a visit to the vet in the first few days after the puppy's arrival. Introductions are a useful means of gauging your vet's approach, as he or she greets and examines your bundle of joy. Exposing the puppy to the clinic at this early stage is also a good way to develop a positive relationship with the establishment, in advance of more traumatizing visits for vaccinations and possibly surgical treatment needed in future.

Initial health check

Many puppies from reputable breeders come with a guarantee of health or 'puppy contract', giving you the right to return them if they are not in perfect health. Whether you take them up on it or not, it is paramount to have a vet check to confirm that your puppy is healthy before you develop a strong emotional bond. Many people become attached as soon as they set eyes on their chosen puppy, which is completely understandable; it then becomes the vet's responsibility to do some straight talking and explain any possible problems when they examine the puppy for the first time.

Vital first visit

Around eight weeks is the time for your young puppy's first visit to the vet. Vaccinations, worming and flea treatment may all be necessary at this age to ensure that your puppy remains healthy and develops normally. Fortnightly checks are recommended by many vets in the early stages to ensure healthy weight gain and avoid any potential health or behavioural problems developing. Your pup's microchip will be scanned and their paperwork checked, so do make sure you bring any and all documents with you.

Getting there

The journey to the vet can in itself be enough to terrify your puppy. Keep them in a specially designed pet carry container lined with soft, absorbent and non-slip bedding and attach it to a fastened seatbelt. If you have an open rear compartment in your vehicle, you can fit a wire cage for your puppy. Alternatively, a larger puppy can be fitted with a harness, which usually has a loop to attach to a seatbelt to prevent them jumping around.

Plan your journey to keep the time that your puppy is travelling in the car to the bare minimum. Exercise them first to get them a little tired; then avoid frightening your puppy by closing doors quietly and driving carefully and smoothly around corners, over bumps and in traffic. If your puppy shows signs of distress, try to divert their attention by providing treats or toys. If your puppy seems very frightened or is sick when travelling in your car, see pages 208–11 for advice.

Making vet visits fun

Create positive associations

Many dogs have an innate fear of the V. E. T., which can make life difficult for you and the veterinary staff. The clinic's evocative sounds and smells only remind them of discomforts suffered on previous visits, so the fear is renewed whenever they come through the clinic doors. To avoid negative associations, give treats and toys before, during and after any visit to the vet to keep the experience as positive as possible. Ask your vet to give your puppy a treat after the examination, and ensure that lots of love is bestowed in reward for good behaviour. Key to productive and relaxed vet visits is the avoidance of immediate response to nervous behaviour and the rewarding of a calm and happy puppy.

Socialize with the staff

Take the opportunity to socialize your new charge thoroughly by allowing veterinary nurses and support staff to approach and interact with them. It is, however, recommended that your puppy avoids contact with other dogs or the floor until after the second booster vaccination is given (see opposite), unless you are absolutely sure that the other dogs have been fully vaccinated. To avoid your puppy developing a fear of the vet, visit the clinic regularly for weight checks or just pop in when passing by, when your puppy can enjoy the experience without being on the receiving end of a sharp needle.

Let's party!

Many veterinary clinics host puppy parties or socialization classes, which consist of a group of up to seven young puppies invited to the clinic for an evening of fun and education. Puppies usually attend between nine and twelve weeks of age, after they have had at least one vaccination. It is an excellent way to socialize your young puppy by meeting other dogs of similar size and age with their owners and veterinary staff, in a relaxed, safe and monitored environment. A puppy party provides your dog with a positive and happy experience of a visit to the clinic. It also offers you the ideal way to be informally introduced to your veterinary practice, the staff and the services they provide, and to learn valuable behavioural and healthcare tips from professionals.

Preventative healthcare

Providing protection

Various measures can be taken to ensure that your puppy is kept safe from potential diseases and parasites that can cause ill health. A young puppy is at the mercy of many harmful infections and pests lurking in their everyday environment, against which they have little defence. The use of preventative medications helps to bolster your puppy's immune system and protect them while they grow into a healthy adult dog.

Vaccinations

These are injections given to your puppy to stimulate their immune system to fight disease. There are many life-threatening viral diseases that infect dogs (such as those listed on pages 60–61) and vaccinations help to produce antibodies to protect your puppy against them. Your puppy is given some protection from these diseases through their mother's milk in the first few hours of life. Colostrum is produced by the mammary glands of mum immediately after giving birth to puppies. Rich in maternal antibodies, it provides essential protection for a puppy up to around twelve weeks of age. Vaccinations are started at six to eight weeks of age, and then repeated at around ten to twelve weeks, to ensure that your puppy is protected before levels of maternal antibodies wane. In some areas or for certain breeds, a third puppy vaccination is recommended.

OLD WIVES' TAIL

I have had dogs for over 20 years and have never had them inoculated, so I don't believe in vaccinations for dogs.

This is an ill-considered conclusion, as the fact that no serious illnesses have resulted is simply pure good luck. The diseases preventable by vaccination are still prevalent today and outbreaks are more likely to occur as concentrations of dogs in built-up areas continue to increase.

Vaccinations are mostly given in the form of an injection under the skin of the neck, called the 'scruff'. Be prepared for your puppy to make a little whimper when the needle goes in, with some puppies experiencing slight discomfort or itching over the site for a few minutes afterwards. Many puppies will feel a little low after their first vaccination – tiredness and poor appetite are common signs over the following 12 hours. If these symptoms persist longer than 12 hours or are more severe, contact your vet.

With the positive effects of vaccination greatly outweighing any potential side effects, annual booster vaccinations are recommended for dogs throughout their lives to maintain strong immunity to these preventable yet potentially fatal diseases. Most vets will send out reminders of your puppy's future vaccinations, but in any case forward-date your calendar to ensure that this important health precaution is not forgotten.

Worming

Intestinal or gut worms are a common parasite in puppies, causing vomiting, diarrhoea, reduced growth and anaemia. An indication of infestation is a puppy licking excessively around their rear end, a pot-bellied appearance or an inability to put on weight. There are at least 12 different species of gut worms known to parasitize the intestinal tract of a puppy, with infections occurring from birth via suckling mum's milk and the puppy's environment. Some of these parasites are transmissible to humans, so keeping your puppy free from worms also helps to protect your family's health.

Medication to treat worms comes in liquid, paste, tablet or topical liquid form, depending on the weight of your dog and the specific worms to be treated. Flexibility is needed when choosing wormers, as some forms can cause stomach upsets in certain puppies. The most effective treatments for all four types of gut worm are available via prescription from your vet; some preparations are flavoured to ensure ease of administration.

The breeder or welfare worker should have given at least one worming treatment to your puppy prior to you taking them home. Generally speaking, intestinal worming should be continued fortnightly for the first three months of life, monthly until six months, and then every three months during your dog's adulthood; your vet will guide you on what is recommended for your area.

The different types of intestinal worm treated include roundworm, tapeworm, hookworm and whipworm.

Roundworm

The most common worm in puppies, this parasite has a similar appearance to a small earthworm, although pale in colour. It causes a pot-bellied appearance in its host and the puppy can seem generally weak with a dull coat and reduced growth.

Tapeworm

This larger, segmented parasitic worm will appear as 'grains of rice' in your puppy's faeces. Attaching itself to the intestine, the worm sheds eggs contained within segments of its body into the faeces and can cause diarrhoea and vomiting in a heavily infected puppy.

Hookworm

Much less common than the above two parasites, this worm is a blood sucker that attaches itself to the canine's intestinal wall, causing bleeding and anaemia.

Whipworm

This least common worm is mainly caught via exposure to the faeces of an infected dog, through digging or when taking your puppy to the park. Once it finds its way into your puppy's intestines, it attaches to the gut wall, causing bloody diarrhoea and weight loss.

Other common parasite problems

Lungworm

This is another parasite present in the UK and shares a lifecycle with slugs and snails. Having infected the host (your puppy) via the ingestion of slugs, snails or contaminated water or vegetation, it moves from the gut through the bloodstream to the heart and eventually lungs, leading to coughing as the mature worms are ejected from your puppy's body. Causing great damage to the lungs, the chance of blood clots and even death, lungworm is a common puppyhood ailment yet easily preventable with many regular oral or topical products.

Heartworm disease

This is caused by the parasitic worm *Dirofilaria immitis* and spread by the bites of certain types of mosquito. The lifecycle of maturity of this worm within the host leads to severe lung disease, heart failure, organ damage and death in many dogs every year. Prevented with the use of either repellents or anti-parasitic medications, this is a condition of warmer climates where mosquitoes are present.

Leishmaniasis

A condition spread by the bite of sandflies and present in many warmer climates of the world where they exist, this protozoal disease causes skin lesions and, potentially, organ damage. Most dogs have cutaneous lesions while others suffer with fever, weight loss, muscle and joint pain or even kidney failure. Leishmaniasis can be prevented by avoiding the areas and times when sandflies congregate; collars and topical treatments can also be used to repel these biting insects from your vulnerable puppy.

COMMON DISEASES PREVENTED THROUGH VACCINATION

Parvovirus

A nasty and incredibly infectious viral disease causing symptoms of severe vomiting and bloody diarrhoea, leading to rapid collapse and death, sometimes within 24 hours. Few puppies survive an infection of parvovirus.

Canine distemper

This highly infectious and contagious disease is often fatal and causes permanent disability and deformity in survivors. With the advent of routine vaccinations, this disease is now rarely reported but has seen a rise recently as vaccination take-up has waned.

Infectious canine hepatitis

Attacking the liver, this virus can cause sudden death in puppies within 24 to 36 hours. Survivors often suffer with long-term liver disease or become carriers, spreading the disease to other canines.

Leptospirosis

Multiple forms of this bacterial disease exist, and are spread by the urine of carrier animals, notably the rat. One form causes acute illness and jaundice; another, a slower insidious form, results in chronic deterioration of the liver and kidneys.

Canine parainfluenza

This is a group of viruses responsible for the highly infectious condition commonly known as 'kennel cough', leading to a harsh, dry cough that can take up to ten days to resolve.

Bordetella bronchiseptica

A bacterial infection associated with canine parainfluenza, causing flu-like symptoms that can dramatically worsen and result in a thick, purulent nasal discharge and chest infection. It is vaccinated against with a nasal or oral spray and is strongly recommended when animals are known to be visiting high-exposure risk areas, such as boarding kennels, dog-training classes or puppy crèche.

Rabies

Endemic to the USA and Southern European nations, this virus is being increasingly vaccinated against as pet travel becomes more widespread. All pet passports and international travel documents require a vaccination against rabies, to prevent transmission of the disease and avoid the need for pet quarantine. A blood test may be needed to prove an adequate immunity to rabies, the sample being taken at least 30 days after the initial rabies vaccination.

Flea control

Visible to the naked eye, fleas are the most common external parasite affecting canines, causing both puppies and owners to itch just at the thought of them! The bites of these blood-sucking parasites tend to cause a mild allergic reaction, making your puppy scratch and leading to skin damage and infection. Fleas also play a role in the transmission of tapeworm between animals and in addition can cause severe anaemia (see page 216) in very young puppies because they can consume up to 15 times their own body weight in blood per day.

Living in the coats of dogs (and cats), fleas can also set up residence in the carpets of heated homes, resulting in bites shared with human inhabitants. With up to 50 eggs produced daily by a well-fed mature female flea during her 100-plus-day lifespan, infestation of your home can rapidly occur unless regular preventative treatments are used. The presence of fleas can be easily detected by looking for specks of black flea dirt (flea poo) within your puppy's coat, or for signs of itching or skin disease.

Treatments are constantly changing to keep up with the rapid development of resistance to traditional medications within flea populations. Prescription-only treatments from your vet, such as topical spot-ons and chews (usually combined with intestinal wormers), tend to be most effective; unfortunately shampoos, some collars, sprays and powders may have only a short-term or limited effect on these irritating insects. Check the label to ensure that the treatment is safe for the age of your puppy, and always use as instructed. If a flea infestation is detected, it is worthwhile treating your home with topical sprays to avoid dormant eggs hatching at a later date.

Tick, lice and mite control

Other common external parasites in puppies are ticks, lice and mites, which can vary greatly in prevalence according to region, climate and breed.

Ticks

Exceedingly hardy blood-sucking creatures, ticks are known disease carriers in certain parts of the world.

Lice

These parasites tend to resemble flaking skin that accumulates behind the ears, causing a puppy to scratch around the head.

Mites

Harvest mites appear as orange grains in the fur and can be extremely irritating. This category also include the mites responsible for demodectic and sarcoptic mange, which burrow into the skin, causing severe skin infection, irritation and disease.

Treatments for ticks, lice and mites can be used in a preventative or post-infection manner. Certain flea medications are known to have an effect on some of these parasites, preventing infections from occurring. Always consult your vet if you suspect a parasitic infection, to ensure that the correct treatment is implemented promptly.

Microchipping your puppy

How it works

Michrochipping is used to permanently identify a myriad of creatures, ranging from horses to tortoises, and the microchipping of a newly purchased or re-homed puppy is a legal requirement in many countries. A microchip is a small device the size of a grain of rice that is placed under the dog's skin, usually between your puppy's shoulder blades. It contains a number that can be detected by a scanner passed over the area where it has been placed. This number is held with your contact details in the microchip company's database and allows a lost animal to be returned to its rightful owner from any welfare centre, vet clinic or government organization possessing an appropriate scanner.

Your breeder or welfare centre will be able to provide you with the information needed to register your ownership with the microchip company involved, which should be updated to reflect your contact details and address as soon as you are able.

Bringing your puppy home

THE FIRST FEW DAYS

Moving to a new environment can be very upsetting for your puppy, but there is much you can do to ease the transition. From day one you should also be starting the processes of toilet training and socialization, as well as learning how your canine communicates. But there will be plenty of scope for fun and games too!

Travelling home

Provide comfort and security

It is best to collect your new puppy in the evening, when they will probably have already been fed and will be naturally drowsy. They should then be settled and with luck will fall asleep on the journey home. Bring blankets or towels with you to wrap your puppy in, rubbing them on mum and littermates before you leave – these smells will comfort your puppy during the drive to their new home and over the coming days.

It is a good idea to transport your puppy in a cardboard box or a pet carry container, lined with a puppy training pad or absorbent paper and a scented blanket or towel. The box or carry container should be secured by a seatbelt for maximum safety, or a passenger can keep firm hold of it. The driver should drive smoothly, taking special care not to disturb the puppy.

Settling in

Take it gently

On arrival home, keep excitement to a minimum, playing with the puppy for only a short while and allowing brief and chaperoned exploration of their new home. Offer a small meal of whatever food they were fed previously, and then give them the opportunity to use either a puppy training pad or the garden to toilet. Finally, introduce your puppy to where they will sleep and attempt to put them to bed.

Surviving the first night

Keeping your puppy near you makes sense, as dogs are naturally pack animals and survive on the comfort and security of others. Imagine being your puppy, taken from their mother and siblings and now in a new place with different sights, sounds and strange people...frightening, right? To help ease this transition, you must take on the role of Puppy Parent, understanding that your puppy will likely cry out for their mum and forgoing a full night's sleep for at least a few days until they settle in.

There is a reason that the term 'pup-ternity period' has been coined – not because it's a new-age fad but because new puppies, just like babies, will wake you up in the night, exhaust you and leave you of little use at work and questioning your sanity.

If you have been waiting a long time for a puppy, then invest in them, taking at least a week off to usher this beautiful new being into your home with kindness and patience. Sleep deprivation and work pressures combined will not make this easy!

My tips for sleep training your puppy are:

- Take time off work for your puppy's arrival – enjoy and revel in it rather than feeling like it's a chore, and allow time for you to rest too!
- Stick to a consistent bedtime – remember that dogs love a routine, so establish one from the start.
- Choose your puppy's new sleeping area –wherever you decide to settle them in the house, sleeping in the same room with them gives your puppy comfort and reassurance as they face this potentially frightening new world without their mum and littermates.
- Don't forget mum – if you are planning to use a crate (which I recommend), think of it not as a cage but rather a comfy and secure den; place a blanket that has the scent of your puppy's mum and siblings inside to reassure your new pup.
- New home comforts – as your puppy settles, it is OK to keep minimal physical contact with them, possibly a hand near them for comfort until they drift off, reducing physical contact over time. If your pup wakes in the night, comfort them with a soothing voice but as little attention as possible, checking whether they have toileted or need to go.
- Pre-emptive toilet breaks – puppies are small, and so are their

bladders, so set a timer to wake them up and allow them to urinate away from their sleeping area. Again, as with a newborn child, having to get up in the night to a youngster with a wet nappy should come as no surprise; but we want to quickly set a night-time toileting regime. Once a puppy realizes that barking or crying for attention wakes you up, this can be a hard lesson to un-learn; so getting up before they do and preventing any vocalizations before they are needed should mean that a good night's sleep can be quickly returned to. Setting an alarm and getting up before your puppy wakes up, initially starting at two- to four-hourly intervals, is a harsh but necessary step towards keeping your puppy comfortable and sleeping quietly while ensuring that you remain in control.

- Distance –after a few days to weeks, your puppy should be walking happily into their crate at bedtime and settling quickly. When this happens, begin to remove yourself from their sleeping area, attempting to extend the length of time between toileting breaks until you can return to sleeping throughout the night. By gaining physical separation from your puppy at a young age, you are endeavouring to teach them the important life lesson that it is OK to be alone, and this will help in the fight against separation anxiety that can develop later (see page 133).

BETTY'S DIARY
Coming home

Day 1 *After bidding her loving breeder goodbye, my beautiful eight-week-old Border terrier puppy and I began our hour-long journey home. She proved to be a good traveller, settling well into her carry container, which was constantly opened during the drive so I could gaze upon my precious cargo.*

On arriving home, Betty waddled around the living room, ate well and played – showing early signs of her brilliance by understanding the concept of fetch on her very first day! When I put her into her crate for bedtime, I prepared myself for whining, as she nestled into her mum-scented blanket in the en-suite bathroom adjoining my room. It was understandable that Betty should be upset at being confined on her own in a strange new place after enjoying the company of mum and three siblings until now. Her whining, though, was worse than I had imagined, and continued for some long hours until I finally cajoled her to sleep with soothing words. Little did I know that the worst was yet to come...

Lessons learned
Be prepared for a bad first night and try to ensure that you don't have to go to work the next day, just in case of sleep deprivation!

Easing distress

The generally recommended approach is to place the puppy in a crate lined with bedding and a puppy training pad for accidents. A heated pad or hot-water bottle tucked into the bedding is also a good idea, to mimic the heat generated by other sleeping puppies and mum. This will help your puppy to feel secure if in another room from where you sleep, and you will be comforted to know that they are contained and safe. A dog-appeasing pheromone product or DAP (see page 206), either sprayed directly onto bedding or in the form of a diffuser, will be very helpful in settling your puppy into their new home.

Playing background music or talking to your puppy softly from another room can help to comfort them without you needing to get up when called. If you do have to go in to your puppy, keep it calm and brief; accept that mistakes will be made on both sides and don't lament over it.

Expect an average of around six hours of sleep a night for the first few weeks. This period will extend in length as the puppy becomes acclimatized to sleeping alone and you both settle into a routine.

Toilet training

Your greatest challenge

The single biggest cause of owner despair during the early days of dog ownership is trying and failing to house-train. Toilet training is a process that requires an abundance of patience. Instinctively, puppies will urinate away from where they sleep, actively performing this behaviour in the wild from around three weeks of age. Dogs in the home environment behave in the same way, so training is needed to teach your puppy that inside your home is a non-toileting zone and outdoors is where they should be going.

First steps

Initially use a puppy training pad, placed in the corner of a room. Some training pads are impregnated with a hormone that, when sniffed by your puppy, will stimulate them to urinate on it. When you are briefly unable to monitor their activities indoors, place the puppy in their crate or playpen to limit where they can toilet, lining it with plastic sheeting and absorbent material for easy cleaning.

It is recommended that as soon as possible after vaccinations allow, you should begin taking your puppy outside to toilet, so that you don't have to train them twice – once to go indoors on a mat, then again to go outside. However, it is not true that a puppy who trains on puppy pads will struggle to learn to go outdoors, and their health and safety should trump a spoiled rug or two when vaccinations are not yet fully completed. The transition can be achieved by taking a soiled puppy pad outdoors to scent mark the garden, or simply present one to stimulate your puppy with the smell that may encourage them to go. Lots of love, attention and even food treats should be given when the puppy toilets in the correct spot, to reinforce the lesson learned.

Planned toileting

Establish a routine of feeding and walking so that you can begin to judge when your puppy is most likely to toilet. Most puppies will defecate within 20 minutes of eating, so you can maximize your success rate by planning to walk your puppy outside around that time. Remembering to take this precaution will help to avoid any accidents, keeping your home clean and, above all, stress free. Most puppies tend to be fully house-trained by around six months of age, although you should be prepared to accept that occasional mistakes can be made up until they are one year old.

Recipes for toilet-training success

Be proactive

Actively take your puppy into the garden or outside area every hour, after eating and drinking, after exercise and immediately on waking and before going to bed. In this way, you can seize the opportunity when they need to go, giving your puppy the best chance to do it in the right spot. Setting a timer means that the entire household can be alerted and involved in toilet training – just make sure that everyone is acting in the same way to keep lessons consistent for your growing pup.

Establish a standard command

Use a command such as 'go wee' when your puppy is going to the toilet. In time, this command will become synonymous with the action of going to the toilet and they will begin going on demand.

Reinforce with rewards

Reward your puppy when they go in the right place, lavishing them with treats and praise to positively reinforce the lesson that going outside is correct. Your puppy gains from performing correctly and begins associating toileting outside with happy, positive feelings.

Learn to read the warning signs

Walking in circles while sniffing the floor is a sure indication that your puppy needs to go to the toilet. Learning to recognize this basic canine behaviour gives you the chance to intervene and walk them outside to wherever you would like them to go before they toilet inside.

Avoid reprimands during or after an accident

Telling your puppy off when they toilet in the wrong place right in front of you is an understandable response, but increasingly it is thought not to work. It can lead to either attention-seeking toileting, where your puppy misinterprets your intervention as praise, or a dog who is anxious to toilet in front of their owners, which makes future training difficult. Also, if caught 'mid-flow' your puppy may not feel the urge to go when carried to the puppy pad or outdoors but may still need to go again soon. Instead it is best just to let them finish, calmly clear it up, and go back to setting that toilet timer.

Don't reprimand your puppy if you find any 'presents' indoors after the fact. Telling a puppy off after the event will only frighten them and possibly cause a setback in all other areas of their behavioural development, because they will have no idea what you are shouting about. It is important to know that your young dog lives in the present, not the past; so misdemeanours that are not seen should not be reprimanded.

If you do spot a rogue poop or puddle, it's a good idea to clean up the mess out of your puppy's sight, as your body language will scream your displeasure and annoyance, which your puppy will be able to detect. Consequently, they will go in more obscure places next time to avoid your wrath. These places will be harder to locate and you will be less likely to catch your puppy en route. Use a biological cleaner to ensure that you remove any scent: less powerful cleaners allow the scent to remain and potentially stimulate your puppy to toilet in that same spot again.

Conversing in canine

Vocalizations

Complementing body posturing (see pages 75–8), the use of vocalizations is an important means by which a dog expresses themselves. Barking, growling, yowling, howling, whining, whimpering, squeaking and screaming all indicate different emotional states, depending upon the pitch of their delivery, and tend to be fairly self-explanatory. Low-pitched sounds are more menacing, threatening or a warning to stay away; conversely, a higher-pitched noise invites the opposite response.

COMMON QUESTIONS
Toilet training

How do I toilet train my puppy when I don't have a garden?
House-training a puppy living in a flat may be more difficult and take a little more time, especially as the first few weeks of life must be spent in the safety of your home. Using a puppy training pad in a low-traffic part of your apartment will teach the basics of toilet training until your puppy has had all their vaccinations and can go out. Walking regularly is then the key to success, finding a small patch of grass near your home for quick access. Bring a section of soiled puppy training pad with you, as smelling the urine scent may stimulate them to go outdoors. Make sure that you thoroughly reward with attention and praise when your puppy toilets where you intended them to go.

I have been trying to house-train my puppy for some time now, and they just don't seem to be improving. What should I do?

In this situation, it is best to consult your vet or a local behaviourist (see page 176). Urinary infections and disorders are uncommon at this early age, but can be the underlying reason why a puppy is struggling with house-training. Alternatively, inherent behavioural problems, such as fearfulness or unconscious mistakes made by you in training, could be causing this slow progress. These issues can be quickly resolved with the help of an animal behaviourist, to avoid toileting indoors becoming a learned and normal behaviour for your puppy as they mature.

Reading body language

What is your puppy telling you?

Although dogs don't understand human languages, they can interpret verbal commands, especially when used in conjunction with a physical gesture. In the same way that our facial expressions complement our spoken words, a dog uses body posture to reflect their feelings. A greater understanding of your puppy will come from a knowledge of basic body language, which is used in canine interactions to defuse physical aggression and foster friendly encounters. It is also important to understand vocalizations, which indicate when your puppy may be frightened, frustrated or feeling in a playful mood (see page 74). Learning to understand the differences between your puppy's senses and your own (see pages 78–9) is also invaluable in helping you to tailor training and games to your new canine companion and to develop the bond between you.

Tail

Originally designed to assist with balance, the tail is the part of a dog's body language that humans best understand. However, a wagging tail is a commonly misinterpreted sign of a contented and happy dog (see pages 241–4 for the five most commonly misinterpreted dog behaviours). In a puppy, a faster wag accompanied by a body wiggle almost certainly indicates a happy and enthusiastic dog in that particular situation. The tail position is also a strong indicator of a dog's emotional state: a tail held high is a sign of an aroused, stimulated canine, while a tail held low or between the legs indicates nervousness, fear or submission.

Ears

Although very different in shape, depending on the breed, dogs' ears are able to transmit a wide range of emotions. Your puppy's ear placement will give much insight into how they are feeling. For example, ears held back or flat against the head signify fear, aggression or submission. Erect or forward-placed ears indicate that your puppy is feeling confident, alert and ready for action.

Eyebrows

The shape and position of the eyebrows can fluctuate. Creased eyebrows and relatively more eye exposed reveal your puppy's anger; relaxed brows and relatively less eye exposed signal a passive emotional state.

Eyes

An important part of human interactions, eye contact is also common between dogs, although it is used very differently in the canine world. A direct stare at another dog is confrontational, questioning dominance or actively threatening. However, most pet dogs learn that a human looking at them in the eyes is not a threatening behaviour. When your puppy turns away their gaze, they are either being politely submissive or just plain bored. Pupil size is also indicative of emotional state. Large pupils are associated with excitement, interest or fear, while constricted or small pupils are more likely in a relaxed and drowsy puppy.

Mouth

The most recognizable dog facial expression known to humans is bared teeth. This is rarely seen in young puppies and it is more the case that you should watch out for this sign in other dogs. It is a sure signal to remove your puppy from the situation. An open mouth with tongue and teeth slightly exposed conveys a relaxed and contented mood, while a closed mouth position is an indication of the dog being alert or attentive. Dalmatians and Staffordshire bull terriers famously reveal their smile to a select few people, although in other breeds a smile can be confused with a fearful grin, which can sometimes precede a bite! Yawning can actually be a sign of stress, so to avoid getting it wrong, behaviourally speaking, check out the section on misinterpreted behaviour on page 241.

Your puppy's stance

Showing how they feel

A puppy's posture varies dramatically, with different types of stance expressing different emotions. The play bow is a common body stance for a puppy, with bent front legs, a stretched back and tail in the air, and a sure indication that they are in the mood for a game. A stiff-legged, upright posture, with the fur standing up on the neck, can indicate fear, arousal or aggression. If your pup lies down with their legs stretched out to the side, they are feeling secure enough to rest in this vulnerable position. Rolling on their back with hind legs raised, head back and soft body posture is the ultimate form of relaxation.

Puppy senses

Sight

In comparison to humans, sight in dogs is surprisingly poor and they are thought to see the world in shades of yellow, green and grey. Darker colours, such as blue, appear more like black to a dog, while lighter colours are seen in hues of grey. Consequently, using blue, red or white toys works best, as they contrast well with green grass.

Smell

Scientists have estimated that a dog's sense of smell is between 10,000 and 1 million times as sensitive as ours and your puppy's sense of smell will never cease to astound you. Dogs have helped their owners for centuries in the search for food by using their highly attuned noses.

Hearing

The biggest difference between your hearing and your puppy's is at the high-frequency range. High-pitched sounds are used in dog whistles to gain dogs' attention at long distances. At levels undetectable to the human ear, high-pitched sounds emanating from the television set, vacuum cleaner or planes can explain why some puppies bark at them. Generally, a dog's sense of hearing is thought to be around ten times as sensitive as ours, which is why many become nervous around loud noises such as fireworks.

Taste

With a sense of taste far less sensitive than ours, dogs are known for having a sweet tooth. They do not share our craving for salty foods, due to a chiefly meat-based diet naturally high in salts. Your puppy must be closely monitored in the home to prevent them accessing sweet substances that can be dangerous. Attraction to sweet-tasting household items such as chocolate, snacks containing artificial sweeteners like xylitol or vehicle antifreeze is common in dogs, and consumption of these can prove fatal (see pages 232–4).

Touch

Dogs use touch in a similar way to humans: to gauge temperature, exert pressure on the body or on things in their environment, and to perceive pain. One of the most important reasons why dogs are such perfect companions for humans is their use of touch to communicate. Strongly associated with emotion, the use of touch is paramount in communicating with your puppy and developing a close bond with them.

How your puppy learns

Lessons from nature

As a pack animal, a puppy's early lessons are learned through play and mimicking other animals in their family group. At eight weeks of age, your puppy has already learned vital lessons from their mother and siblings and is now ready to be moulded into the dog you would like them to be around people.

Hierarchy in the wild pack is crucial to individual wellbeing. Each member knows their own place and works with the others as a team, without aggression, in order to maximize the pack's chances of survival. Understanding the importance of exerting dominance over your puppy without the need for physical punishment is supremely important to ensure a calm household and a contented dog.

Wild dogs rarely vocalize, using body language to converse with each other. For humans, however, verbal communication is much more important, so the use of verbal commands with obvious physical gestures is the best approach when teaching your puppy what you would like them to do.

Rewards for good behaviour

Attention and affection must be earned and considered as much of a treat as a dog chew. If it helps, think of your puppy as a demanding child – giving them attention for bad behaviour will only encourage them to act in the same way again. Only reward good manners and calm behaviour, ignoring bad behaviour and mistakes. This can be tough! Use food rewards where necessary to enable your puppy to understand when they have behaved correctly.

Trial and error

A common learning process in canine behaviour, as in human behaviour, is trial and error. In this way, your puppy can begin to appreciate the relationship between a behaviour and its consequence, either positive or negative. Learning from mistakes and gaining positively from success are powerful tools that you can use to train your puppy. For example, a puppy that is only given attention when quiet will quickly realize that barking leads to an affection deficiency.

Playing with your puppy

Establish mutual trust

Play is a crucial element in your new puppy's development and an excellent way for you to form a strong friendship with them...and surely one reason you got a dog in the first place, right? Playing regularly with your puppy will enhance their willingness to please when it comes to basic training. It also reinforces in their mind the concept that people are sources of fun and entertainment, leading to a more sociable, happy and well-balanced adult dog.

Play helps to overcome your puppy's fear of the unknown, encouraging confidence by diverting attention away from aspects of their environment that may have previously worried them, such as other dogs, cars or joggers. Exercising their intellect and natural instincts, game playing stimulates their senses and burns off some of that excess puppy energy until they can safely venture into the great outdoors.

Remain top dog

Wild-dog puppies will play fight with each other in a battle of will and strength to assert their position in the hierarchy. Bearing this in mind, any game instituted with your puppy must result in you winning the majority of the time and keeping hold of the toy in question. This teaches the puppy very early on who is boss, setting boundaries of behaviour that they will need to adhere to in order to stay in favour with you.

Outlaw rough play

An important aspect to remember is that you are playing human–dog games, not dog–dog games, which involve the use of teeth. Any rough play, such as directly pushing your puppy, scuffling on the floor or encouraging biting or grabbing of hands or clothes (whether intentional or otherwise) should be banned. These types of activities can stimulate your puppy to bite. However soft and harmless it may seem at this early stage, rough play starts a pattern of behaviour that can become dangerous at a later stage. If your puppy's teeth come in contact with your skin during any activity, even accidentally, immediately cease the game to teach them that biting means no more play.

Puppy games

Tug-of-war

This well-known game is enjoyed by many puppies, but is one that must be carefully considered. Always win more encounters than you lose, otherwise your puppy will believe themselves to be stronger than you and may challenge your authority. Once you have won, the toy used in the game must be kept from the puppy and put out of reach, otherwise they will believe that they have won the encounter and kept the prize.

Never pull too hard or lift the puppy from the ground with the toy, as this can damage their teeth or mouth. If your puppy becomes overly aroused or is very strong-willed, this may be a game to avoid altogether.

Treasure hunt

This enrichment game uses your puppy's superior sense of smell to hunt down food treats placed around the home for them to find. It is an entertaining game that all puppies will love, but hound dogs elevate it into an art form. Searching for food is a natural instinct in all dogs and this game encourages your puppy to put aside any fears they may have and explore their environment in pursuit of a tasty treat.

Start by placing the treats while your puppy watches you, giving them a command such as 'find' or 'seek' before letting them loose. Once this has been mastered, make the game more difficult by hiding treats and toys around the home or garden without them watching. Some toys can be bought impregnated with a scent, while others, such as Kongs, can be covered with a liver spray available from pet stores or filled with edible treats. This simple yet rewarding game encourages the intrepid explorer that is inherent in all puppies and will dramatically increase their confidence in – and enjoyment of – your home. Some canine behaviourists and trainers suggest never feeding your dog from a bowl and habitually feeding them this way, reducing boredom and encouraging natural foraging as a way to counter anxiety in modern pooches.

Fetch

A favourite since dogs were first domesticated, a game of fetch can be enjoyed with your puppy from their arrival at your home. Although fetching is an inherent ability of gundogs such as retrievers, all breeds can be taught to fetch and this will bring added interest to walks in the future.

Start by tossing a rubber toy to gain their attention. When the puppy picks up the toy, call them back and offer a treat when they return it to you. In order to pick up the treat, puppy will need to drop the ball, so use the verbal command 'drop' when they perform the required action. Food treats can soon be phased out, as playing the game becomes reward enough in itself, with all the fuss and attention that the puppy receives when returning with the tossed item. Avoid using the traditional stick for this game, as it can splinter, lodge between the teeth or be swallowed – something we see in veterinary clinics a lot! It is safest to use tennis balls or rubber toys.

Socialization and habituation

Build confidence

Both socialization and habituation are important processes identified by animal behaviourists as means of helping a puppy venture forth confidently into a domestic environment.

Socialization

A socialization programme will teach your puppy how to recognize and interact with their own species and all the other species they come across in everyday life. Socialization with humans and other dogs is vital for your puppy's development, teaching them social skills, dispelling fears and encouraging a relaxed and well-balanced temperament in all environments.

In order to help socialize your puppy, begin to introduce them as soon as possible to the different people and animals listed below. (Bear in mind the restrictions on mixing with dogs of unknown vaccination status prior to your puppy completing their full course of vaccinations at ten to twelve weeks.)

- A variety of people of different ages and sex: men, women, young children in prams and pushchairs, older children and elderly people
- People in different outfits: wearing hats, glasses, costumes, uniforms, helmets and masks
- People moving or travelling in different ways: running, walking, on scooters, bikes, rollerblades and skateboards
- A variety of animals: other dogs, cats, horses, livestock, small mammals such as guinea pigs and rabbits, and other pets such as tortoises (always keeping your puppy under control to avoid a dangerous situation developing)

Habituation

Habituation is the process of accustoming your puppy to non-threatening objects, environments and experiences so that they learn to ignore rather than fear them. Exposing your puppy to a variety of objects and places in a calm, patient way will encourage exploration and help to prevent irrational fears from developing.

Start with everything found in your home until puppy can go out for walks when their vaccinations are completed, then begin exposing them to all the potentially frightening things that inhabit the great outdoors. It is vital for the new puppy parent to avoid comforting the puppy when they display irrational fear of objects that they have been exposed to. Allow time for your puppy to calm down and begin investigation, responding with encouragement, praise and affection when they do so.

Help to habituate your puppy fully by exposing them to the items on the following checklist:

- Novel environments: friends' houses, veterinary clinics, bus stops, railway stations, shopping malls, parks and playgrounds
- Novel objects: cars, bicycles, household appliances such as the vacuum cleaner, mobile phones, children's toys and new puppy toys
- Novel sounds: thunderstorms, children's screams/cries/play, fireworks, traffic, aeroplanes and trains
- Novel experiences: being groomed, being examined by you and the vet, being picked up, being rolled over, going for walks, going on public transport, travelling in cars, in lifts and on escalators, and being left alone for short periods of time

Meeting cats

Control their contact

If you already have a cat and decide on a feline–canine union, ensure that you have the means to separate the animals from each other and respect the fact that the cat was there first and, if frightened or cornered, can badly injury your playful puppy. A baby gate, playpen or crate works well to segregate an over-exuberant puppy, with a scratching post or basket kept out of reach for the retreating feline. If they have to be left alone together, always keep your puppy in a secured area so that the cat can choose to interact with them or keep well away. Introduce your puppy to your cat at an early age and chaperone any interaction so that you can moderate behaviour on both sides before the puppy gets over-excited or the cat becomes fearful or aggressive.

Manage meetings

Keep meetings brief and always allow your cat a chance to escape, reserving a room or two of the home as a puppy-free zone. Restrain your puppy but not your cat, so that the latter can choose their proximity to the new arrival and your puppy cannot give chase. Reward both cat and puppy for good behaviour when interacting with one another.

Problems can occur when you have a confident puppy that likes to bounce and lunge at the cat, since they know it will then run and provide something to chase. If this happens, distract your puppy with toys and treats so that you – rather than the unimpressed feline – are always the focus of games and fun.

Be patient and understanding

In most cases, puppies will quickly learn respect for housemate cats – the superiority complex of a feline is useful in teaching a puppy good manners. When raised with cats, most dog breeds will learn to accept them. Slowly, your cat will become used to the puppy smell and, as long as a concerted effort is made by all family members to give your feline the same affection as is lavished on your puppy, your household should eventually become a calm and happy one. Just be prepared that your cat may never call your puppy their friend!

Meeting other dogs

Find some neutral ground

If you decide on a new puppy in addition to an existing dog, the first meeting is best staged on virgin territory for both dogs and in an environment guaranteed to be disease free. A good site might be a friend's house or garden with no other dogs or an area of your own home where your resident dog has not previously ventured, such as a bathroom or bedroom. Choosing neutral ground will mean that your current dog will not feel the need to exert territorial behaviours or guarding aggression, and will be interested in the puppy for curiosity's sake.

Oversee the meeting

Exercise both dogs well before the meeting and then allow them to interact with one another, keeping a close eye to ensure that all remains calm and the meeting is positive. Toys and food can be a source of potential conflict, so pick up all your older dog's toys before the puppy arrives and make sure that you have separate toys and feeding positions for each dog.

Provide a refuge

It is a good idea to use a playpen, crate or baby gate when introducing a puppy, as this will give your older dog some respite from the puppy and also allow safe investigation of each other through the protection of bars. Don't leave the dogs together unsupervised for at least the first month of ownership, until you are sure that they are sound canine playmates.

Meeting children

Give them guidelines

When you are introducing a puppy to children, always discuss the correct way of treating them beforehand so that the children are not overly rough or inadvertently frightening. Explain that excited behaviour such as squealing, screaming and running about can be very scary for your new arrival and may also stimulate unwanted chasing behaviour in some puppies. Children should be dissuaded from picking up puppies as they tend not to support them properly, which can result in discomfort and upset for the puppy. Keeping the puppy on the ground will ensure that they and the children are all comfortable and can play together in safety.

Stress the need for rest

Remind children that a puppy needs lots of sleep and tell them not to wake them up, as this will result in an irritable puppy that will not appreciate their attentions. Allow the puppy timeouts by giving them a playpen or crate in which to play or sleep on their own and consider providing a new game or hobby for the children to distract them from smothering the new arrival. After a few weeks, the novelty of a puppy tends to wear off as both puppy and children settle down to life together.

Ensure contact with kids

If you don't have any children, it is important to expose your puppy to them wherever possible. Some puppies raised in adult-only environments can find children frightening and, without adequate socialization, can in some cases develop nervous or aggressive behaviours towards them as they grow. The high-pitched squeals of a young child combined with uncoordinated grabbing and running can not only frighten dogs but also trigger prey instincts in those not raised with them. Invite friends or family with children to interact with your puppy, or introduce them to children in the park so that their social development includes establishing relationships with young people or at least not being fearful of them.

Insurance

Why it is important

Pet insurance is fast becoming standard practice in dog ownership, with one in three canines needing veterinary treatment every year. Available from a number of different providers, pet insurance will protect you from large, unexpected veterinary bills incurred when your puppy is unwell, injured or even the cause of an accident.

Choose your policy with care

Always read policies carefully, as making a choice purely on the basis of cost may result in you falling foul of exclusions or cover limitations should your puppy become ill. Choose a policy that provides 'cover for life', which means that the provider will continue to pay claims for ongoing conditions for the entire life of your pet. Many providers offer annual policies that will stop paying claims after just one year of treatment for a specific condition.

This may leave you without further opportunity to re-insure your pet for that illness with a competitor, as it will be classed as a pre-existing condition.

Get advice

Pet insurance generally follows the rule 'you get what you paid for', so seek advice from your vet and your dog-owning friends before making a decision about a provider.

Grooming

Establish a routine

Grooming your pet is similar to the behaviour that animals perform on each other in the wild. While its primary purpose is to clean, grooming also plays a role in strengthening the bond between owner and dog. Grooming is also an opportunity to give your puppy a regular all-over health examination. Starting a grooming regime from an early age helps a puppy to accept being handled and examined before grooming becomes an essential part of their day-to-day care as they grow.

Coat care

Your puppy's fur will need brushing or combing, stripping or trimming, depending on their breed and coat condition – for example, a Border terrier's coat is stripped, while a poodle's is trimmed. For the more involved grooming techniques, it is best to start by visiting a professional groomer, then consider taking lessons or ask a breeder's advice as to how you can do it at home. The long-haired breeds, such as the Old English sheepdog or chow-chow, need to be groomed daily with a brush or comb. Brushing in the direction of hair growth will provide the most comfortable experience for your puppy.

Regular brushing and checking of the skin also gives you the opportunity to look out for early indications of dermatological conditions, such as redness of the skin, flaky skin, loss of fur, discharge, infection, lumps or lesions, as well as external parasites such as fleas and ticks.

Nail trimming

It is important to keep your puppy's nails trimmed in the early stages, when they will be unable to wear them down naturally on walks in the outside world. You need to seek expert advice from your vet or professional groomer before attempting this at home. A blood vessel and nerve run through the centre of the nail, which can obviously bleed and cause pain if cut into. Use a pair of purpose-designed nail clippers available from a pet store or vet clinic. If you don't feel confident about doing nail trimming yourself, ask your vet to show you how (many vets will offer a nail trim at the first vaccination) or visit a professional groomer. Grinding tools are becoming increasingly popular for newbie dog owners to help take the sharp ends off a puppy's nails, helping to keep them short without the risk of bleeding or pain.

Oral hygiene

Your puppy's baby (deciduous) teeth will fall out consistently from around three to six months of age, when they will be replaced by adult teeth. Nevertheless, during this early period it is important to introduce your puppy to teeth cleaning, so that they become accustomed to the procedure. This will facilitate future dental care that can prevent dental disease occurring later in life. Daily brushing is recommended, with regular checks by both owner and vet to ensure that there are no aspects of your growing puppy's dental health that need addressing. Dental disease is thought to affect around 40 per cent of dogs as early as three years of age, so purchasing and using toothbrushes, flavoured toothpastes and dental chews will keep your puppy's teeth and gums healthy and future vet bills down.

Ear cleaning

Waxy deposits can accumulate in dogs' ears (more often in dogs with floppy ears), causing a musty odour and potentially leading to more serious ear infections. Get into the habit of checking your puppy's ears regularly; purchase ear cleaners from your vet and seek professional advice on how to use them safely. Cotton wool and liquid cleaners tends to be the most effective method – but avoid cotton buds, which may inadvertently cause pain or injury to your puppy.

Bathing

Choose a mild puppy shampoo from your vet clinic or pet store and bathe your puppy by supporting their head above water and massaging in the shampoo while keeping it clear of eyes and ears. Rinse with warm water, then towel dry in a warm environment to prevent your puppy becoming cold.

Shampooing your puppy regularly can dry out their skin and strip away the coat's natural waterproofing, so bathe them only when they are dirty to a level that cannot be dealt with by brushing alone. Monthly bathing is the most frequent that a healthy coat will tolerate, although more regular bathing is required if a puppy is suffering from a skin condition. Many dogs need bathing only a few times every year and just need a good wipe down when smothered in mud, to keep them clean without drying out their skin.

Monthly diary

Over the coming chapters, you will find a diarized guide to a developing puppy. You don't need to read them all at once – this is not a test! Just work through them month by month as your puppy grows, using the 'Problem puppy' and 'Sick as a dog' chapters (see pages 169–211, 213–40) as go-to guides to reassure yourself if you come up against any behavioural or health concerns on the way. More than anything, don't be too critical of yourself if mistakes are made: that's everyone's experience of parenting! Just reflect, adapt and take things step by step to enjoy this once-in-a-lifetime experience. Dogs feed off our emotions and are incredibly intuitive, so remaining a calm, relaxed and joyful puppy parent is key to bringing up a calm, relaxed and joyful dog.

Weeks 8–11

THE HAIRY TODDLER

This is an adorable stage, when your endearing addition to the family is full of energy and enthusiasm and many misdemeanours are quickly forgotten. Be mindful that bad behaviour allowed now will only become more of a problem when your puppy is older and bigger. So this is the time to establish good behaviour and eliminate the undesirable.

8–11 weeks: Owner checklists

What your puppy may do

- Night-time waking, crying and soiling
- House soiling
- Play biting and clothes pulling

- Chewing and minor destructiveness
- Chasing of other animals and children
- Crying when left alone
- Jumping up
- Being fearful of everyday objects around the home

If you experience any of these, refer to the 'Problem puppy' chapter on pages 169–211 for advice.

What you should do

- Set house rules from the start and stick to them
- Consider baby gates and crates
- Be a fair, reassuring guide
- Start basic training and play with your puppy
- Keep nutrition simple
- Avoid startling your puppy or coddling them when fearful
- Attend a puppy socialization class
- Socialize your puppy with different types of people

All of these need to be done by the time your puppy is 11 weeks old.

Health reminders

- Daily cleaning to ensure puppy is kept in a hygienic environment
- Have an initial health check with your puppy's new vet
- Vaccinations are due at eight weeks and then at ten to twelve weeks
- Give a worming treatment fortnightly
- Provide flea treatment
- Insure your puppy

Parental duties

Begin socialization and training

Your puppy's keen senses will be put to full use when they arrive home and are bombarded by all the many sights, sounds and smells of their new environment. Just like a human toddler, your puppy will be into everything in an attempt to explore and experience the exciting new world around them. This is a very important time for your puppy's social development and the establishment of their relationship with their new family.

It is easy to get caught up in the joy and wonder of owning such a sweet and loving creature. You may fail to realize just what a crucial learning stage this is for them, which is why it is the perfect time to start basic training. Although your puppy has a short attention span at this age, the lessons learned (either good or bad) will be difficult to modify later. This is so much the case that some believe a puppy not taught to fetch at this age, for instance, will be unable to develop the suitable skills to be a guide or detection dog later in life.

Take first house-training steps

Both bladder and bowel control will have improved considerably from when puppy was with mum, so now it's about teaching them when and where it is OK to go.

Your puppy's behaviour

Encourage exploration

Curiosity and a desire to explore are tempered by a general fear of everything, so positive encouragement of exploration will avoid possible phobias that may come to haunt your puppy in adulthood. In nature, puppies of wild dogs approach unknown objects with great caution, but with subtle support from their mother in exploring them, they quickly come to accept them.

This measured approach to socialization is important – but the balance between being overprotective and too compelling can be difficult to achieve. Don't force exposure to new things; just let it happen naturally while avoiding the temptation to over-parent, as this can lead to a fearful adult. Allow puppy to be exposed to something for long enough that either they overcome their fear on their own and then investigate its source, or you improve the situation positively by diversion with treats or toys.

Assess their puppy personality

Your puppy's individual personality will begin to shine through, so see if you can tell whether they are assertive or shy, strong-willed or eager to please. One of the joys of dog ownership is that no two dogs are ever the same. If you try to understand your dog's special character, you will gain a better appreciation of exactly what is needed to train them into a well-adjusted adult.

PAWS FOR THOUGHT
Coddle, reassure or ignore?

When human children are upset or frightened, the normal response is to hug them, talking softly to reassure them that everything is OK. We can converse verbally with other humans, enabling us to rationalize complex situations and overcome fears with words. This is not the case with your puppy.

Of course, we must offer reassurance at times of stress and upset; but we must be careful not to mirror those same anxieties ourselves, and instead offer a calm and relaxed persona in these moments, ignoring the non-threatening stimulus and remaining confident and positive.

You should not correct or chastise your puppy either, as this will upset them further. Coddling is not recommended, with excessive love and affection in those moments leading to potential for confusion and a worsening of their anxiety. This is a tricky tightrope to walk with your puppy. Just remember that your role as puppy parent is to guide and advise, protect and educate, fighting any of your own feelings of nerves or anxiety on the journey that your intuitive pooch may easily absorb. Dogs feed off our emotions, so don't feed the negative ones!

Whatever the stimulus, use the techniques of desensitization and counter-conditioning (see page 188) on whatever is evoking the fearful response in your puppy by using treats and praise as encouragement as they confront and overcome them. When your puppy shows greater resolve and confidence, shower them with rewards and praise to reduce or dispel their fears and replace them with positive feelings and confidence.

Develop a puppy social life

Socialization with people and other dogs is essential during this life stage. Seek out puppy-socialization classes (or 'puppy parties') in your area until the vet says that it is safe for you to take your puppy to the park to meet older canine buddies. Invite friends and family around so that the puppy is exposed to different types and ages of people, including children. These interactions are important for the puppy, not only to appreciate their place in the world but also to learn basic lessons such as control of biting, physical coordination and how to play.

What your puppy may do

Behaviour that needs understanding

New owners must expect waking, crying and soiling during the night. They need to be very patient and appreciate that their puppy is still very young (see toilet-training advice on pages 70–73). Crying when left alone is common, as your puppy is unused to being separated from the affections of their owner, mum or siblings. A human child would behave the same way, so we need to show understanding and limit such time apart as much as is humanly possible. Fearful behaviour towards everyday objects can seem amusing, but this needs careful monitoring and understanding so that your puppy doesn't develop irrational fears and instead becomes a well-balanced adult dog in all situations.

Behaviour that needs counteracting

Play biting and clothes pulling are things that puppies tend to indulge in and owners facilitate, but both should be dealt with quickly. Chewing is a completely foreseeable problem at this stage, while your puppy investigates their new environment; only minor destructiveness will result, as their jaw is yet to attain full strength. Jumping up and chasing (especially other animals in the house and children) may cause alarm until your new recruit learns the rules of polite society.

What you should do

Feeding

Keep nutrition simple by choosing a good-quality food and sticking to it. Mixing or changing foods of different protein sources will upset your dog's gut, causing diarrhoea or excessive wind. Offering lots of different foods to your puppy to suit their changing tastes will only lead to a picky dog.

Training

Constantly remind yourself that your puppy will soon grow up, so don't allow any behaviour, such as jumping up, that may be difficult to cope with when they get bigger. Trial the collar and lead indoors and begin with simple commands. Above all, play with your puppy to keep training sessions fun and positive. Be a consistent and fair parent by setting house rules and keeping your patience while enforcing them, to correct unwanted behaviours before they become bad habits. Chewing on shoes, urinating in the house or biting that is overlooked as 'cute' at this stage may be hard to eradicate as your puppy grows older.

Family life

Watch out for disharmony in your home, as a new puppy in the house can cause jealousy between sibling children jostling for their affections. Other animals in the home can feel understandably upset by the arrival of a new family member, leading to aggression, a lack of appetite or hiding. Ensure that the whole brood is carefully watched over during this hectic, disruptive time.

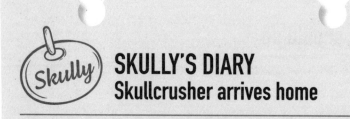

SKULLY'S DIARY
Skullcrusher arrives home

Day 1 *After eight weeks of Skully being cared for by mum and her owner's family, the time had come to bring her home. She immediately stood out to me as one of the more confident puppies, coming up to me, my wife and children and interacting with us all on our many visits as she grew. We have a busy family home and, when choosing a puppy, I also needed to keep in mind our current dog, Betty, who was a little older and had suffered a back injury the previous year, meaning she was slower and frailer than before. Skully seemed calm and not overly bouncy, with a mixture of breeds all known for being calm, intelligent and easy to train. With my priorities more divided and oversubscribed since Betty's puppyhood, we needed a dog less challenging than my Border terrier had been – and Skully was to be the perfect addition to our family.*

On getting home, she calmly approached Betty, who sniffed her at first and then began to be a little more interested in this funny little fluffball. In time, Betty actively started to play with Skully, which was the first time we had seen this perky part of her personality since her accident and surgery. Skully showed a little nervousness at being introduced to the big black furry thing that sauntered into the garden to take a look at the new arrival. Known as Rickets, our cat showed the puppy little interest and an immediate degree of deflated acceptance after being consistently let down by our continuing need to introduce more animals and children into his abode. The children were all immediately in love, playing with the new arrival as I chaperoned and kept an eye on the situation to make sure Betty didn't feel left out. Naming this new puppy came to a democratic vote, and the children decided that this little pom-pom of a pooch should have the name Skullcrusher (they were watching the film How to Train your Dragon on repeat at the time). My wife showed strong opposition to this ridiculous name while I saw the incredibly funny side and our children outvoted us – yet we were all able to agree on the toned-down name Skully...Still, my wife has yet to forgive us.

COMMON QUESTIONS
Habituation

My German shepherd puppy hates the vacuum cleaner. As soon as I turn it on, he barks, urinates and runs off. How can I help him to get used to it?

A vacuum cleaner is a frightening device to a wary puppy. It has a high-pitched whistle mixed with a low grumbling sound and lunges forward suddenly, then retreats – a very aggressive and threatening monster! Start by allowing your pet to explore and sniff it when it is off, placing a treat or two over the machine to encourage them to come closer. Once you can repeat this several times and your puppy is comfortable, you can attempt to turn it on while it is stationary and at a distance or in another room. Follow the same process, using lots of treats and praise, then hopefully, with time, your puppy will be less fearful of this noisy everyday appliance.

OLD WIVES' TAIL

You should give your puppy milk, as they are still young and miss their mum.

No, you shouldn't. Weaning is an important part of the growth process and eight-week-old puppies should be on solids by the time they leave the breeder and mum. Also, a dog mum's milk is low in the carbohydrate lactose, which many puppies cannot tolerant. When given cows' milk, which is high in lactose, many puppies develop diarrhoea.

Social development

Avoid startling your puppy – from eight to ten weeks of age they are very prone to developing fear, so keep all new experiences positive and non-threatening. Attend a local puppy-socialization class – these are great fun and highly educational for both you and your puppy. Socializing with other dogs and people is very important, so don't just sit at home enjoying your beautiful new playmate on your own. Organize play dates with other puppies, have friends around, take your puppy out in the car and expose them to everyday life and all those things that are routinely encountered.

Health reminders

Safety precautions

During this time your puppy must be kept in safe environments (for example, the home, garden and vet clinic). Avoid exposure to other possibly unvaccinated dogs until at least a few days after their second vaccination (around ten to twelve weeks). This is because your puppy does not develop an active immunity to the diseases protected against after the first vaccination alone. To achieve active immunity, your puppy needs the booster vaccination.

Vet visits

Puppies can become very frightened of various experiences at this stage of their development and they can carry that fear with them for life. If the first appointment with your vet is traumatic, your puppy may never want to visit again. (Think how Betty and Skully felt with their dad being a vet!) Take food treats and a toy along with you when you visit the vet so that the rewards for going to the clinic outweigh the negatives, encouraging your puppy not to fear these necessary trips in the future.

Preventative treatments

Vaccinations are due at eight weeks and then again at between ten and twelve weeks, depending on the product used by your vet. Worming medication should be given every fortnight at this age. If your puppy is going into your garden, it is a good idea to administer a flea treatment. You can obtain a topical or oral flea treatment suitable for your puppy's weight from the vet.

Health problems

Diet alterations make diarrhoea common in the early stages of puppy ownership. Your puppy's gut has to become accustomed to new foods slowly and the stress of changes in their environment. If the diarrhoea persists for more than 24 hours or there is any blood or worms present, contact your vet.

Microchipping and insurance

Ask your vet to scan your puppy's microchip to make sure it is functional and registered with the company in your name and with all your current contact and address details. Insure your puppy for their protection and your peace of mind, doing your research to ensure the best cover possible (see page 89).

Basic training at home

Rewards of early training

Even at the tender age of eight weeks, your puppy is an eager student waiting to be taught the finer points of life with humans. Basic training is a great way to communicate with your puppy, fostering in them a sense of themselves and their place in the world while also tiring them out and leading to better sleep. Training will enhance your relationship with your puppy and establish good habits early, to give structure and boundaries to their new environment and avoid the development of undesirable behaviours that may be difficult to modify later. Training results in a grown dog that will be calm, well behaved in all situations and safe, responding quickly to commands.

Rules of engagement

Follow this checklist of basic rules to govern all your interactions with your puppy:

- Be consistent – start with a strict set of house rules and stick to them.
- Be patient – your young puppy has a limited attention span, so lessons need to be short and frequent.
- Be positive – give excessive amounts of praise when your puppy does the right thing.
- Be fair – accept that mistakes and accidents will happen; never resort to physical punishment.
- Be rational – accept that you are human and will make mistakes, lose your temper and wonder what you have done wrong. Every puppy parent feels the same at some point; so ask for help or take a break and soon these feelings will pass.

Training principles

Puppy training must always be kept short and interesting, using simple commands starting with your puppy's name. Have treats and lots of attention at the ready to reward the puppy when they do something right. Do not repeat commands more than a few times, as they will become noise without meaning. Avoid giving commands in harsh tones, as this will decrease the likelihood of your puppy responding to them.

To reinforce the training, assign a hand gesture to go with each command. Trainers have varying hand gestures for different commands, so it really doesn't matter which one you use as long as you are consistent. To avoid confusing your puppy, make sure that the whole family uses the same gestures and verbal commands. Getting all members of the household to practise the simple training exercises on pages 108–9 at different times of the day for just a few minutes each time is key to achieving the best results.

PAWS FOR THOUGHT
To pick up or not?

If your puppy is in obvious danger, picking them up is of course appropriate. In all other cases, allow your puppy the chance to assess the situation for themselves and often the initial fear reaction will be replaced by interest...followed by boredom! For example, picking up a puppy that quivers when meeting a friendly child is not a good idea; instead, reassure with words and also guide the child as to how best to interact with your puppy. Rather than giving your puppy physical attention in these moments, divert their attention with a toy while getting the child to stroke them using soothing tones or offering a treat.

Basic training exercises

At this age you can begin to teach your puppy basic skills, such as walking on a lead, come, sit and stay, as well as the 'good dog' and 'no' commands. With time and patience, these can be fine-tuned to allow your grown puppy to compete in obedience trials or sporting competitions, or simply not to be a liability when out and about in the human world.

Come!

1 Using your puppy's name, crouch down with open arms and call them to you. As you do so, you can offer a treat as an enticement.

2 When they come, hold their collar, then reward puppy with lots of affection and the treat. In your garden use other family members or friends to restrain them, calling puppy to you from greater distances to test their responses both on and off the lead in a safe environment.

Walking on a lead

1 Before you start venturing out to the park, your puppy should have been exposed to the lead at home. Burn up some excess puppy energy with an active game, then offer them the chance to sniff and examine the lead before attaching it to their collar.

2 Using a treat to keep your puppy's attention on you and not the collar, ask them to come with you, ensuring that you keep the lead slack. If they pull, immediately stop and call the puppy back to you so that they quickly realize that pulling on the lead doesn't get them anywhere. Don't allow chewing of the lead when walking, as this annoying habit can lead to problems in later life.

Sit!

1 Gaining your puppy's attention with a treat, get them to come close while looking up at you. Keep hold of the treat and let their nose touch it, then slowly move it up and back over puppy's head towards their tail. If their front legs remain on the ground, they should naturally sit as their back end sinks towards the ground.

2 Say your puppy's name and 'sit' as their bottom touches the ground, then reward with a treat and lots of fuss. If they stand up on their back legs or move backwards, you may be moving the treat too high or fast. Later, progress to using a hand gesture, rewarding your puppy when they sit by crouching down and giving them attention or a tasty morsel.

Stay!

1 With your puppy in the sit position, stay close and say their name and the 'stay' command. Keep still to prevent them confusing your movements with a command to move, rewarding puppy if they remain in place for ten seconds. With practice, gradually increase the time period in the sit position and try to make slow, deliberate movements away from your puppy while still facing them and saying 'stay'. If puppy remains in place, return to them and give them a treat. Gradually increase the 'stay' time and the distance you move away.

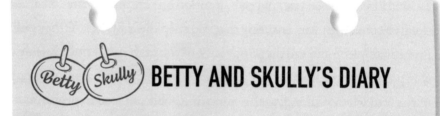

BETTY AND SKULLY'S DIARY

Betty was very strong-willed and, even as a puppy, everything was a battle. She took a long time to become used to the crate, with night-time crying a regular occurrence for the first few weeks. Skully on the other hand was a delight, although having a big sister to keep her company and show her the ropes was definitely a massive help. I did not set alarms at night time for Betty and paid the consequences for it, with accidents of all varieties that she seemed very keen to bathe in. Being on my own at the time, and pre-children, the lack of support, sleep-deprivation resilience and patience led to mistakes made; yet despite them Betty developed into the most amazing, well-behaved and adaptable pooch I could wish to have. With time, consistency and understanding, I was able to learn from my mistakes with Betty early on, and this led to Skully's puppyhood being a far less stressful (and disgusting) experience.

Lessons learned

Puppy parenting is a team effort, and with my wife, children and Betty all playing a part, Skully has been a dream dog from the very start. Of course, there will be differences in early development based on breed and individual personality – Skully was definitely a pup who understood the use for training pads and respect for belongings where Betty did not. With experience and age I have definitely evolved in my training methods over the years, from using more disciplined methods to those of increased positivity, reassurance and understanding, and have reaped the rewards as a result. We all need to accept that we make mistakes – we are but human – though we must remain open and able to learn from them to become better people and pet parents.

Weeks 12–15

THE JUVENILE DELINQUENT

Finally your puppy can venture into the great outdoors and expend some of that boundless energy. Many trainers believe that this stage is key for owners to establish good behaviour and self-confidence in their charges. With the 'cute factor' wearing off over toileting mishaps and chewed belongings, your puppy will begin to challenge you, so be prepared for some patient parenting (and screaming into pillows!).

12–15 weeks: Owner checklists

What your puppy may do

- Still struggle with toilet training
- Be fearful of everything
- Question your authority

🐾 Take all attention away from other pets

If you experience any of these behaviours, re-read the appropriate sections of the book and reassess your approach.

What you should do

🐾 Be patient with toileting accidents and be better at reading the signs of needing to go

🐾 Train your puppy indoors, outdoors and in puppy classes

🐾 Ensure attention is given to your other animals

🐾 Enforce some puppy alone time indoors when you are home

🐾 Keep nutrition simple

🐾 Avoid startling or coddling your puppy

🐾 Be a vigilant puppy chaperone in all environments and interactions with other dogs and people

If you are unable to tick off any of these tasks, you know what to do!

Health reminders

🐾 Second vaccination/booster due, plus possibly the rabies vaccination

🐾 Worming and flea treatment suggested

🐾 Bathing or grooming may be needed

🐾 Teething common at this stage, so offer lots of toys to prevent your puppy chewing belongings

Parental duties

Puppy guide to the outside world

Once their vaccination course has been completed, the job of exposing your puppy to the amazing and potentially frightening outside world begins. This major event may bring an increase in behavioural problems such as fear and aggression. All the socialization and habituation completed indoors must be moved outdoors with greater intensity and variation. Gradually, your puppy should be given the opportunity to experience the sights and sounds of motor vehicles, crowds and other dogs.

Your puppy's behaviour

Prepare to be challenged

Your puppy will start to test you, questioning your authority and asserting themselves physically and emotionally. Some puppies may show stubbornness or aggression in the process of clarifying their place in the hierarchy of your pack, while others will more readily accept guidance. A structured home life with clear routine and strict rules will ensure a relatively painless transition through this period.

Avoid playing rough games that teach your puppy to challenge or even bite you, as you are not their sibling or equal but their guide and protector, whom they should never be encouraged to challenge. At this stage you must appreciate that although early signs of aggression may not be as dangerous as in an adult dog, you should implement a zero-tolerance policy now to avoid worrying behaviours becoming the norm.

Prepare for a backslide in training

Your previous good work on the training front may seem to be going backwards as your puppy enjoys their independence and selectively ignores commands. With all the captivating smells, sights and sounds of the outdoors combined with their new-found freedom, puppies of this age need gentle but firm reinforcement of commands and training to ensure that they are kept on the right track. It is worth considering enrolling in training classes at this stage (see page 122), which offer advanced lessons designed to stimulate your puppy and underline the message that you are the parent.

 PAWS FOR THOUGHT
Playing rough

Many owners – and if I'm honest, especially us males – like to play rough with their charges, thinking that this is just another entertaining game or, more worryingly, that it will 'toughen up' their puppy. This type of activity may seem fun to us, but constant physical tussles can teach your puppy to look for this type of rough play in any situation. In the wild, just a growl from a senior dog will avert an altercation with a rival, without the need for a physical fight. When you play rough or a tug-of-war game, your puppy sets themselves against you in a battle of will and strength, which spawns questions as to who is the strongest. You should always win more games of tug-of-war than you lose, putting the toy away after the win to keep the coveted item when you notice your dog getting a little overly excited.

In some dogs, rough play can leave them feeling aroused or over-stimulated, sometimes extending to mouthing and biting. Even the softest of bites should be swiftly dealt with, to prevent them from becoming acceptable behaviour and to avoid the potential for actual bodily harm. A firm, low-growled 'no' should be uttered immediately, followed by a short period of starving your puppy of attention to dissuade them from this potentially dangerous behaviour.

It does seem as though the early stages of puppy training are all about what you can't do with your puppy. But time will reveal that lessons learned early within a strictly developed social structure result in an obedient adult dog that is able to experience more of what the world has to offer than if they were unruly.

What your puppy may do

Behaviour that needs understanding

Some lucky owners will already be enjoying a fully house-trained puppy, but occasional accidents are generally still to be expected indoors.

In new encounters with the outside world, your puppy may show fearful tendencies in the form of wariness of strangers, children, crowds, traffic noise and other dogs. If you are unlucky or do not manage to read the warning signs (see page 241 for the section on commonly misinterpreted behaviours), your puppy may also become a victim of canine aggression outdoors. Remember that no interaction is better than a negative one.

Behaviour that needs counteracting

Destructiveness is common at this age, with your puppy becoming stronger, taller and able to reach a whole new variety of playthings. Their increased activity and energy levels can lead to boisterousness, chasing and aggressive play fighting with children and other animals. Your puppy may begin to question your authority, ignoring you or barking when given commands or growling at you when playing with toys. You are not the only one whose frustration levels may rise – other animals in your household may also show signs of irritability and stress as a result of the new arrival.

SKULLY'S DIARY
Skully decides that she really, really loves baby's dummies (pacifiers).

Day 41 *At the time, my son was just three and still enjoyed the dummies that were then discarded all over as he made his way around the house. Skully, it seemed, shared his affection for them, constantly grabbing them and chewing the teat with her sharp baby teeth, rendering them unusable. One particular day my wife spied her chewing one and went to take it away, only to have Skully protest, run and then swallow the newly chewed-off teat in one gulp.*

After a sheepish call to me at work, my wife headed down to the practice, where an X-ray confirmed what we already thought: the teat was in Skully's stomach. I wanted to avoid surgery on such a young pup, so decided to induce her to vomit in the hope that we could encourage the rather large teat to make a return journey and be brought up without the need for a scalpel. On the third vomit, Skully fortuitously brought up the teat, with my wife and me never more grateful to investigate and clean up a large pool of sick.

Lessons learned
Puppy-proofing needs to be modified, updated and consistently policed to avoid medical mishaps from befalling your investigative young canine.

What you should do

House-training strategies

Be patient with persistent house-wetters and avoid cleaning up in front of them. Angry body language is easily detectable by your puppy and will result in them finding more obscure places to toilet indoors.

If puppy is successfully using training pads at this stage, decrease their use or remove them completely to encourage a greater confidence in toileting outdoors. A common mistake is to coddle a puppy by continuing to allow them to toilet only indoors without actively teaching them to go outside. Limiting a puppy to one toileting spot and one medium, such as a training pad, up until the end of this period will result in resistance to the use of others, such as grass or flowerbeds. If your puppy is solely conditioned to associate going to the toilet with being inside on a training pad, even when taken for a long walk outdoors they may hold on until they find themselves back indoors on familiar territory.

Simply having a garden and leaving the door open doesn't mean that your puppy will learn to use the outside rather than going indoors, however. Put puppy on a lead and walk them outside, spending time with them so that you are there to reward them with treats and praise when they go.

If puppy is still making multiple daily mistakes, keep as calm as you can and take positive action. Put yourself on 'wee watch', setting an hourly alarm during waking hours to encourage pup outdoors. Monitoring your puppy's habits to gain an understanding of when they toilet, such as after drinking or before bedtime, will give you an early warning to get them outdoors. Actively walk your puppy outside or place them on training pads during those regular toileting times in an attempt to give puppy the ability to go correctly in the right spot. Always remember to reinforce the action positively with treats and praise, to ensure that the lesson is well learned.

Outings and social development

Never feel embarrassed to ask owners of fully grown dogs if their pet is aggressive towards other dogs before you allow your puppy to interact with them. If your puppy is getting over-excited or you are concerned about the possibility of aggression, extricate them from the situation using lead pressure and verbal commands. When your puppy comes to you, reward them with treats and attention to finish on a positive note. Remind yourself of canine body language to help avoid potentially calamitous dog encounters.

Conversely, don't smother or coddle your puppy – remember that they are a dog and need to learn about the world at a dog's normal eye level. If you don't give them some freedom at this stage, your puppy may never gain the tools to develop out of being fearful or shy. Walks are also important in teaching puppy to accept being on the lead, using a long lead to increase their sense of freedom while you flex your training muscles.

Don't forget other members of the family. Give any other dogs or cats the attention they deserve in order to avoid jealousy or aggression. Consider keeping your puppy restricted to certain parts of the house at times so that the other animals can get some peace.

PAWS FOR THOUGHT
Training people

One thing I noticed during Betty's training was that in some respects she would behave for me and not for others. I was reminded of the way most people are unwilling to reprimand naughty children when their parents are nearby. This human trait seems to hold true when applied to other people's dogs: a visitor to your home will be reticent about scolding a misbehaving puppy when you are present, so in most cases you do the reprimanding for them, which does not work as well as if they had done it themselves.

This is a complicated social situation, as dogs are social animals, needing instruction from all members of the group to learn and develop. Betty jumping up was a terrible problem with visitors, although I quickly taught her that she would gain no attention when jumping up to me. Visitors would let her do so, however, and even actively encourage it, not appreciating that jumping up is a bad habit. My reprimands to get down then fell on deaf ears.

Be prepared to impart your knowledge to others so that your puppy receives the consistency of instruction they need from all interactions. Make sure everyone uses a command such as 'down' or 'no'. Most importantly, when your puppy performs the correct response for guests, encourage them to reinforce the lesson with lots of praise or a treat.

Training

Consider enrolling in training classes during this stage to challenge your developing puppy (see pages 126–9) and improve both your and their social network. You should also keep training them using basic commands at home, both indoors and outdoors.

Start teaching your puppy that life with humans involves some separation and alone time. This is an important lesson, similar to the one children learn when they discover that going to school involves being away from their parents for periods of time. Begin training your puppy to be comfortable on their own by leaving them for short periods when you are still in the house. Placing puppy in a crate for a nap, using a playpen enriched with toys for some activity, or keeping them in one room using a baby gate when eating all encourage a puppy to feel comfortable without constant attention at paws' reach. If you can get your puppy used to being separated from you for short lengths of time while you are at home, gradually extending the time up to one hour, this will allow you the freedom to then venture out for quick errands without concern.

Health reminders

Preventative treatments

Monthly worming until six months of age is recommended using oral liquids or pastes for smaller puppies and tablets or topical liquids for larger ones. Apply a flea treatment monthly to avoid any flea allergies developing. Ensure that it is administered at least 48 hours after bathing, as most treatments require a healthy amount of sweat present on the skin to be effectively absorbed.

Health checks and routines

Check between toes and in the eyes and ears after every walk for foreign bodies such as grass seeds and twigs – a puppy isn't adept at removing them on their own.

Diarrhoea can be a problem at this stage too, now caused by eating undesirable items in the park. Be vigilant and learn which parks have the least amount of scraps left lying around.

Your puppy will begin teething now, so provide them with lots of interesting toys to chew to help alleviate the discomfort.

Consider giving your puppy their first bathing or grooming session, plucking the ear canals if need be to keep them clean and clear.

Travel requirements

If you are interested in travelling abroad with your puppy or live in a country that has rabies, get their first rabies vaccination completed after the age of 12 weeks.

Park life

Make it mutually enjoyable

As a puppy owner, you will develop a new appreciation of local parks as your puppy is allowed to venture forth into the outside world. During this exploration, you will expose them to many potentially frightening experiences, including new environments, dogs and strangers. When common sense prevails, most fear-evoking scenarios can be comfortably negotiated so both of you are able to enjoy your outings in the park.

The first walk

A long-awaited event in most new-dog households, walking your puppy outside in public for the first time is an exciting experience for all. It is highly rewarding to watch your puppy's reactions to things and to show off the latest addition to your family with parental pride. Your puppy will be experiencing so much for the first time, so it is your job to ensure that all these experiences are positive. A negative experience or meeting involving aggression is worse than no meeting at all.

Possessing a basic knowledge of canine body language will allow you to preside safely over the first walk and to avert any unwelcome incidents. Your puppy's initial nerves or fears are understandable responses on this big day, and can physically manifest as barking, hiding, freezing, trembling or holding their tail between their legs. Allow your puppy the chance to overcome any nervousness without your intervention, as prior knowledge will tell you that, given a few moments to assess the situation, a puppy tends to shed their nerves and assume a more robust attitude.

Always keep a collar and ID tag on your puppy, as is mandatory in many countries, and potentially use a harness alongside it for larger or more boisterous pups. Always use a lead in public places, as it is preferable that your puppy is restricted rather than being able to run away from you in excitement or fear. A long lead will give them freedom to explore while you maintain control.

Meeting other dogs

Making friends with other canines is important in order for your puppy to learn dog etiquette, so that they don't develop fear-related aggression and aren't perturbed by the variation in canine sizes and shapes. Ask the owners if their dogs are friendly with other dogs before allowing your puppy to get close. Don't assume that all big dogs can't be trusted, as it is more likely that your puppy will be attacked by a dog of similar size and stature than an obviously larger, more dominant adult. If you have friends with calm dogs, start there, not forcing your puppy to interact but reassuring them in these situations and allowing them to build up social confidence over time.

Place your puppy on the ground with lead attached and crouch down to allow them to retreat beneath you while you gently ward off the other dog, reinforcing your position as protector and guide. When your puppy seems ready, tell the owner to let the other dog approach on the lead. Not all the dogs you see should be approached, as that can sometimes lead to a reactive and frustrated pooch who can't understand why they cannot meet every dog they pass. Other dogs on leads should be approached with caution, as they can be on a lead for a number of reasons, including being nervous, aggressive, blind or recovering from surgery. Remember that dogs on a lead cannot move freely or naturally, which can result in nervousness or irritation, and it is commonly reported that most canine altercations occur when at least one of the two dogs meeting is on a lead.

Meeting other people

People generally love puppies and will be eager to meet your adorable young charge when you are in the park. Although it is important to expose your puppy to all the shapes, sizes, colours and ages of other humans, early meetings should be calm and gradual.

Ask any strangers who want to meet your puppy to approach slowly, allowing the puppy to sniff their hand before stroking. If your puppy seems nervous, ask people not to stare directly at them. Direct eye contact in many species is challenging, so it can be a little threatening to your puppy. Most maturing puppies will overcome this perception, realizing that humans look each other in the eye without wishing to engage in conflict. This can be achieved at home by giving your puppy a treat while looking them in the eye and smiling. If you use this approach, puppy will gradually begin to recognize the range of human facial expressions that are associated with positive actions.

Puppy training classes

How they will help

Training classes are fun, informative and rewarding experiences for both you and your growing puppy. They vary greatly in structure, style and content, although obedience training is the most common type. It is well understood that many new puppy parents are not experts when it comes to canine behaviour, so classes are designed as much for training new owners as they are for training puppies. Classes will also help to address and correct any behavioural problems that you may be concerned about (see the 'Problem puppy' chapter on pages 169–211).

Choosing a class

Ask the advice of other dog owners and your vet to find one that is reputable, even attending a few different classes without your puppy to choose the best one. Small classes of around five puppies, in which the participants remain the same every week to ensure consistency of training, are the most effective. Puppies should also be of similar size and age for socialization exercises to be most beneficial for all involved.

BETTY'S DIARY
Our first argument

Day 40 *Betty has just grown tall enough to jump onto my expensive leather couch. However cute it is to see her ambitions finally realized, I swiftly condemned her actions and told her to get off. For the first time in our relationship and in true tantrum style, she began to bark at me. I replied with a firm 'no', only to be peppered with little testing barks and scampering theatrics. My first reaction was one of amusement – though I quickly put my dog-training hat on, appreciating that this was the first sign of rebellion and needed to be calmly managed. I again retorted 'no', then, holding her collar, walked Betty into her crate, where she remained for five minutes. After her time out, I released her in silence, then gave her attention when she sat on command a minute later, things calmly returning to normal.*

Day 41 *Repeat offender! I left Betty for a few minutes to go and get some milk at the local shop. When I returned she was lying resplendent on the sofa, chewing a sheepskin cushion with the smug satisfaction of a \juvenile delinquent. 'Get down,' I demanded and she leaped off the couch at pace.*

I then sat down to examine the saliva-stained cushion, when again she started to bark at me. 'No,' I replied, but she continued to bark and leap about. I repeated myself, but to no avail, and she was returned to the crate for another well-deserved time out. I realized that she was feeding off my annoyance by barking louder and at higher pitches, so promised myself that next time, one 'get down' and the correct response in Betty would be the end of it. Later that afternoon she again perpetrated the unthinkable, launching herself onto the couch. I countered with a formulaic 'get down,' which to her credit she did. Betty then started with the barking again, but this time I ignored her, and quite quickly she lay down in silent protest.

Lesson learned
Patience, consistency and understanding your puppy's individuality are crucial in order to maintain a calm household.

Undesirable training methods

Avoid any class that uses force or punishment as a quick-fix solution. This type of aversion therapy may get an immediate result but could lead to behavioural problems in your puppy later in life.

Socialization stage

After choosing a class that meets your needs and suits your lifestyle, arrive early to allow your puppy to settle after the car journey. Astute trainers will assess each puppy that joins the class and determine its needs based on temperament. A good dog trainer tailors the class to suit the character and disposition of each puppy-and-owner pairing. Most classes begin with a play period during which the puppies are allowed to socialize together under the watchful eye of the trainer. Any excessive force or aggression will be quickly quelled by the trainer to avoid fearful responses and to keep proceedings positive.

Training strategies

The next step is the demonstration of basic commands by the trainer with each puppy, at times rather annoyingly gaining a quick response to a command that has previously brought you little success. Most training strategies involve understanding your puppy's point of view in a given situation and reacting accordingly to affirm a positive response.

How you can benefit

Your trainer will have an excellent understanding of canine behaviour and body language and will be able to use this knowledge to train a puppy to do what they want when they want it. As the weeks pass, the classes will teach you these skills and give you the opportunity to ask questions in a supportive environment to improve your understanding of the canine mind. A training programme will generally be given to you as you leave, with at-home exercises and owner tuition designed to help you mould your growing puppy into a calm, well-behaved adult.

Weeks 16–19

TEENAGE REBELLION

This period sees all the attributes of a teenager come to the fore. Willingness to run from authority, experimenting with stealing and exhibiting antisocial behaviour, poor manners and selective deafness can make you question your decision to get a dog. Growing out of the cute and cuddly stages, these longer, leaner and stronger versions are designed to test the patience of even the most Zen puppy parent. Consistency is the key to success, with skills learned in the past being heavily called upon to survive this trying period.

Weeks 16–19: Owner checklists

What your puppy may do

🐾 Misbehave in your presence and when left alone

🐾 Bite the lead, bite others or bite you

🐾 Resent being groomed or examined

🐾 Be fearful of new things and even regress in confidence

🐾 Have the occasional toileting accident indoors

If you experience any of the above, you have a normal puppy on your hands. If you are dealing with all of them, you need to consider reaching out to local behaviourists or dog trainers for help.

What you should do

🐾 Summon your patience to remain fair and consistent

🐾 Don't allow your puppy to get away with bad behaviour

🐾 Acclimatize them to being alone for up to three hours

🐾 Keep puppy stimulated with different toys, walks and activities

If you tick all these boxes, you are smashing this puppy-parenting business, but if not, that's OK; it's still all achievable.

Health reminders

🐾 Worming and flea control are again needed

🐾 Keep your puppy's nails in check by walking on rough surfaces or learning to trim them

🐾 Grooming procedures such as bathing, teeth cleaning and general checks should be routine

🐾 Expect loss of teeth over the next few months

Parental duties

Be vigilant in monitoring behaviour

A strong bond will have developed between you and your puppy by this age, helping you to bring problems under control with patience, understanding and love. Having jumped many behavioural and training hurdles to get here, you should not become complacent. With self-confidence increasing, your puppy will not be so eager to please, resulting in an occasional battle of wills that can last many months. More complicated behavioural problems, such as fear aggression or separation anxiety, may just begin to manifest themselves and must be addressed swiftly, otherwise your puppy (and you) may be destined to live with them forever.

Be persistent in their development

Just like a human teenager, your puppy may not appreciate being restrained, cuddled or groomed at this stage. It is important to persist in your efforts to encourage the examinations and assessments necessary for the ongoing health and wellbeing of your puppy that they find irritating, to ensure that these healthy practices will be sufficiently tolerated in the future.

Your puppy's behaviour

Prepare for volatility

Your puppy can exhibit a distinct duality of character at this stage, being sweet, well-trained and attentive one minute and then crazed and ignorant the next. Although your puppy would like you to believe that they are a full-grown adult, they are far from it. Understanding this, you need to keep your puppy well under control to avoid actual bodily harm,

133

while also allowing them enough freedom to make mistakes and learn from them.

Reassess their developing personality

Your puppy's personality is being fine-tuned now; displays of increased shyness or over-exuberant boisterousness are aspects of behaviour that need addressing. It will become obvious whether your puppy is assertive or withdrawn in nature, with each personality type bringing with it both positive and negative attributes. Conflict or nervous, fearful aggression may have reared its ugly head, which can cause a puppy parent to feel embarrassment or despair.

The breed of your puppy will begin to have its effect on their personality, with the genetic heritage of the working role for which their ancestors were specifically bred resulting in both interesting antics and behavioural conundrums in the home environment. More complex training can be attempted to channel new-found independence or skills, tailoring this to suit the particular attributes of the student while avoiding any under-valuing of house rules or respect for fellow family members.

Watch out for fearfulness

Fear can again be evident in this month of life, with your puppy harbouring the desire to run from any real or perceived threats that they encounter. Maintaining the balance between continued exposure to new individuals and environments and protection from fear-related situations can be challenging. Don't be afraid to seek out experts in the fields of behaviour, training and veterinary medicine to ensure that any difficult behaviours exhibited at this stage are dealt with correctly.

What your puppy may do

Declare their allegiance

Despite all your teenage puppy's rebellious behaviour, they will by now share an obvious bond with you and your family, which somehow manages to cancel out all the bad points.

Behaviour that needs understanding

Your puppy may exhibit new fears of things they have been exposed to previously, with fear of traffic, new environments and nervousness around strangers added to the mix. They may start to resent being groomed or examined and still have the occasional toileting accident indoors. Chewing should be on the decrease, although your puppy will become bored of old toys and increasingly destructive if these are not regularly substituted for new ones or if their exercise needs are not met.

Behaviour that needs counteracting

Your puppy may experiment with ever more elaborate ways to break the rules in your presence and may also misbehave when left alone. Barking, destructiveness and soiling can all be early warning signs of over-attachment or separation-anxiety disorders that can plague your puppy into adulthood. Biting of the lead, other people, animals and even you may occur during this testing period. These behaviours need to be corrected immediately.

Some puppies will have been trusted off the lead in the park with mixed results – many will run off to play or begin scavenging for any discarded edible morsels, appearing as though they have been forever deprived of proper meals! With growing stature and self-confidence, your puppy may begin stealing food from plates or develop mild food-related aggressive tendencies towards other animals or people, including you.

What you should do

Day-to-day discipline

Continue to be a good puppy parent by exhibiting fairness and consistency. Don't let your attention to training and house rules wane and start allowing your puppy to commit minor misdemeanours. Ensure that all members of the house are following the same rule book, as different rules from different people will confuse puppy and lead to mixed results for each individual. Never allow biting or aggression and be sure to discuss any problems that you are having with your puppy with other family members to collate information, vent frustration and keep tension and annoyance levels down within the household.

Keep a close eye on the problem if you have seen any evidence of aggression or nervousness in your puppy. If the situation appears to be worsening or cracks are beginning to appear in the puppy-parenting unit, talk to your vet regarding possible referral for specialist behavioural advice.

COMMON QUESTIONS
Behaviour

When my puppy really misbehaves badly, is it OK to give them a light tap across the hindquarters or nose to make them understand how naughty they've been?
Physical punishment should *never* be used. Physically reprimanding a puppy to teach it discipline is an archaic method still used by some today. However, behaving in this way will only break the bond of trust and friendship that you have developed with your puppy,

▲ Border terrier Betty with new addition Skully, a mix of three breeds all known for being calm, intelligent and easy to train. She stood out to me in her litter as one of the more confident puppies and introductions between the two dogs were fairly calm, with Betty showing a renewed playfulness in the company of the new pup.

Basic training exercises

◄ COME!
(see page 108)
Crouch down
and call your
puppy with open
arms. You can
offer a treat as
an enticement.

► When they come, reward
them with lots of affection.
In your garden, call them to
you from greater distances
to test their responses both
on and off the lead.

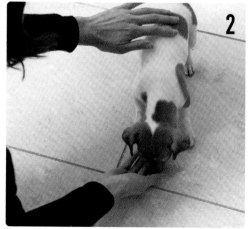

1

◀ WALKING ON A LEAD
(see page 109)

Before you start venturing out to the park, your puppy should be exposed to the lead at home. Offer them the chance to sniff and examine the lead before it's attached to their collar.

2

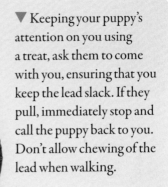

▼ Keeping your puppy's attention on you using a treat, ask them to come with you, ensuring that you keep the lead slack. If they pull, immediately stop and call the puppy back to you. Don't allow chewing of the lead when walking.

SIT! (see page 109)

▲ Gaining your puppy's attention with a treat, get them to come close while looking up at you. Let their nose touch the treat, then slowly move it up and back over their head; they should naturally sit if their front legs remain on the ground.

2 ◀ Say your puppy's name and 'sit' as their bottom touches the ground, then reward them with a treat and lots of fuss. Later, progress to using a hand gesture with the command, rewarding your puppy when they sit by giving them attention or a tasty morsel.

STAY (see page 110)

▶ With your puppy in the sit position, stay close and say their name and the 'stay' command. Keep still to prevent them from confusing your movements with a command to move, rewarding puppy if they remain in place for ten seconds. With practice, gradually increase the time period in the sit position and the distance moved away.

Problem Solver

◄ MOUTHING AND AGGRESSION (see pages 170–5)
A degree of mouthing and mock-aggressive playful behaviour is to be expected in a young, confident puppy. But biting or aggression in adult dogs can have serious ramifications and must be dealt with swiftly.

► OVER-EXCITEMENT
(see pages 177–80)
A small puppy that constantly jumps up in exciting situations can be endearing, but this behaviour can become a nuisance in an older, heavier dog. Children in particular need some guidance in how to handle this.

◄ MOUNTING
(see pages 181–3)
Trying to mount another puppy or person is fairly normal canine behaviour and in most cases is not sexual. Burning off your puppy's excess energy through exercise can be one solution.

► EXCESSIVE VOCALIZATION

(see pages 184–9)
This behaviour is more common in smaller-breed dogs, and attention-seeking is the most usual cause. Tips for prevention include increased exercise – a tired dog is a quiet dog – and giving attention only when your puppy is quiet and well behaved.

◄ CHEWING

(see pages 190–93)
Chewing should be expected throughout your puppy's life, even well into adulthood. It is best that your puppy feels confident enough to chew in front of you so that you are able to control what they have access to!

► HOUSE SOILING

(see pages 196–200)
Remember that your puppy is likely to continue making the occasional toileting mistake up to six months of age and beyond – patience with toilet training is crucial.

► NERVOUSNESS AND FEAR

(see pages 201–7) Socialization and habituation are key in nurturing your puppy into a calm and confident dog. Neither coddle nor condemn your puppy for nervous behaviour, but give them the chance to overcome fears on their own.

◄ TRAVEL SICKNESS AND CAR PHOBIA (see pages 208–11)

A car journey can be a frightening experience for a puppy, but slow and steady exposure to car travel can help, as well as performing simple actions to reinforce the association of car travel with pleasure, such as playing with your puppy after a short journey.

Basic health check (see pages 28–9)

Eyes These should be bright and fully open, with no discharge or redness, as this can indicate disease.

Gums These should be pink, indicating that the puppy is healthy and not anaemic from worms or ill health.

Skin and coat A shiny coat free of dandruff indicates a healthy dog. Patches of hair loss and scabbing lesions could indicate fungal infection or external parasite infestation.

Genitals and anus Males should have two testicles descended; if not, the puppy is classified as cryptorchid and requires surgical treatment to correct the condition. Females should have a clean vulva. Both sexes should be checked for any diarrhoea staining around the anus, which could indicate gut upsets, worms or early digestive problems.

Ears Check that there is no wax build-up in the ear canals and no smell evident, which could indicate infection. Check the pinnae (ear flaps) for skin disease.

Umbilicus (belly button) Check that this is flat; a swelling near this site can indicate hernia and may need surgical correction.

Feet and nails Dogs have five toes on the front feet and generally four on the back, occasionally with a dewclaw (the functionless remnant of a big toe) on the inside of the hind leg. All nails should be intact and unbroken.

Common puppy illnesses (see pages 216–21)

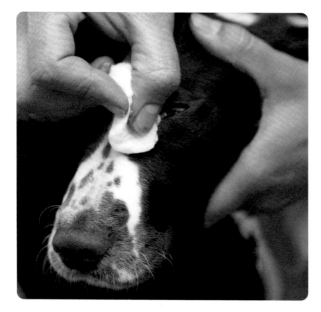

◀ Injury and infection are the most common cause of eye problems and require a visit to the vet. Dark brown- or red-tinged discharge from the eyes on a daily basis, however, is normal and, like 'sleep', can be cleaned away from your puppy's eyes with moist cotton wool.

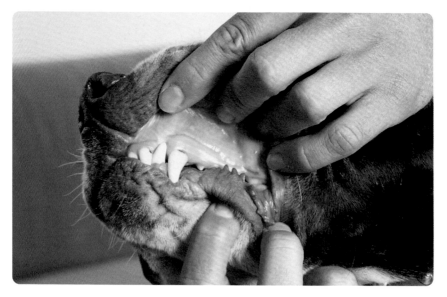

▲ Checking your puppy's teeth and gums regularly and training them to be comfortable with this examination is essential in keeping their oral cavity in pristine condition. Bright pink gums are a sign of good health; pale or white gums could indicate anaemia.

▲ Check your puppy's ear canals daily for foreign bodies or signs of infection. Regular cleaning with cotton wool and an ear-cleaning preparation is highly effective in keeping wax levels to a minimum and reducing the chance of infection or parasite infestation. Checking inside your puppy's ears daily after walks can prevent the need for painful removal of foreign bodies.

First Aid – Resuscitation (see pages 229–30)

▶ Lay the puppy on their side with their neck extended and their head slightly lower than the rest of the body. Check the airway for obstructions, clearing out any saliva or debris from the mouth with your hand (if your puppy is a victim of drowning, you should remove the water from the lungs by holding them upside down). Assess if the puppy is breathing by watching their abdomen, which should rise and fall, or place a piece of hair or grass in front of their nostrils to see if it moves. If there is no sign of breathing, you may need to resuscitate your puppy by using artificial respiration.

1

2

▶ Close your puppy's mouth by holding their nose with one hand while extending their neck. Make a tube with your other hand and exhale a puff of air through the nose to expand puppy's chest at a frequency of 15–20 times per minute (once every 3–4 seconds).

Warning You should use expired air resuscitation and cardio-pulmonary resuscitation only as a last resort, if professional help is not available, as the techniques can lead to injury of your puppy or yourself. These hints are not a substitute for professional assistance or proper study of first aid.

◀ Remove your mouth after each breath and check for signs of breathing. It is also important to check for a heartbeat, either by gently squeezing over the heart to feel its beat directly or by checking for the femoral pulse. The heart can be located at around the point of the elbow in relation to the chest on the left side. The femoral artery is a large artery found on the inside of the back legs thighs and is easily palpated in dogs for the assessment of their pulse.

3

▶ If you are certain there is no pulse, commence CPR. Firmly squeeze the chest at the point of the elbow, making 15 compressions per 10 seconds (for an average-sized dog) to stimulate the heart to begin pumping again. Two breaths exhaled through the nose, as in Step 2, should follow in quick succession. Repeat the cycle for one minute. Check again for breathing and pulse every minute. Once the puppy is breathing on their own, dry them off if wet and keep them warm. Seek professional assistance as soon as possible.

4

▲ IN AN EMERGENCY (see pages 224–5)

Try to stay calm if your puppy is injured or harmed, and think before you act. The first step is to remove your pup from any immediate danger, using a thick towel or blanket (or, failing that, a jacket or coat). Contact your vet immediately.

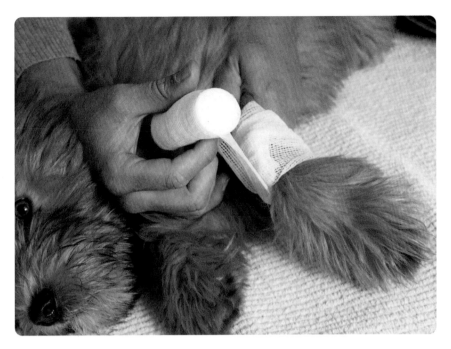

▲ EXTERNAL BLEEDING (see pages 225–6)

If your puppy is bleeding, apply pressure over the site with your hand or a bandage, adding another bandage on top if blood seeps through. Don't apply a tourniquet. Try to keep your puppy quiet and still while you call your vet.

▶ NURSING YOUR PUPPY

(see pages 222–3)
Only in severe cases will your puppy be kept at the vet's clinic. At home, provide a warm, quiet place for them to recover and pay close attention, monitoring their eating, drinking and toileting habits to ensure they are recovering as expected.

▲ BURNS AND SCALDS (see page 227)

Take first-aid measures similar to those you would use for humans in the event of burns or scalds – apply a cold compress or immerse the area in water for approximately ten minutes, if possible. Keep your puppy warm, as burns can, counter-intuitively, lead to hypothermia, and use saline-moistened dressings on the affected area. Avoid medication until you have sought your vet's advice.

leading to a fearful individual that may develop aggressive tendencies towards you or others in the future.

In the heat of the moment people can react rashly. A good puppy parent should always pause for a few seconds to think about the situation and respond in a calm, appropriate way to avoid undoing all their good work and potentially scarring puppy for life. In most cases, physical punishment will teach a dog nothing more than how to avoid being hit in the future – they will continue to behave badly, but avoid you.

A type of physical punishment that was commonly used in the past is 'rubbing a puppy's nose in it' when it has inappropriately urinated or defecated indoors. This reaction will simply frighten your puppy, as they live only in the moment and will not understand your anger at past indiscretions; it can even result in a puppy developing a taste for faeces! Be honest with yourself and know your limitations; if you have had a testing day or feel that your patience is low, keep training to a minimum that day and offer up a stimulating walk instead, providing your puppy with appropriate chew toys and treats when you get home to facilitate a relaxed, carefree evening.

Training

Train your puppy to be left for a period of up to three hours, making as little fuss as possible at your departure. Selectively ignore puppy for 15 minutes to keep things calm and relaxed before you leave, and provide toys, food and water in a secure and temperate part of the home. Take longer and more interesting walks now that your puppy is calmer and better behaved on the lead. Continue with training classes and home lessons, such as teaching tricks.

You can also learn more about your particular breed of dog, finding out what they were originally bred for and like to do, so that you can nurture their inherent abilities. For example, the Border collie is a herding dog, so will be very good at fetch and other hide-and-seek games. You can even try teaching this breed to dance, since it requires good agility, another excellent ability of a Border collie. But they do have a high herding drive for animals and people, which can be annoying...no one's perfect!

To lead or not to lead?

There comes a time in any young puppy's life when you want to try them off the lead. The timing of this event is a point of much debate and greatly depends on your puppy's individual development and your training regimen. A lead is the only thing that stands between your puppy and potential danger, so it must remain in place until you are certain that their responses to commands are reliable or the environment that you release them in is safe and secure.

If in doubt, try a long lead, which will give your puppy a sense of freedom and provide a lifeline if they prove themselves unworthy. In areas free of entanglements, such as a field with no dogs or other animals, children or elderly people around, these leads can be used to test out basic commands when your puppy is nearing readiness to be let off lead. Make a point of being animated on walks so that you are the most interesting attraction in the park, using treats and praise to guarantee your puppy's quick return to you. Continue practising basic commands at home and in the garden to hone their recall skills, trialling them off the lead outdoors when there is nothing obvious around to divert their attention away from you.

BETTY'S DIARY
Terror and the terrier

Day 79 *I was working at a veterinary clinic beside a huge field, so in my lunch break I took the very excited Betty for a walk there. She was a fetch legend at this stage (having shown early signs of prowess on her very first day at home). I found myself to be the only dog owner in sight so, distancing myself from the road and entrance, I let Betty off the lead. I threw the ball numerous times, with Betty returning it, dropping it and receiving a treat for her good work.*

I then allowed her to sniff around on her own, as I noticed three young boys walking back from the tennis courts on the far side of the field. As they were walking straight for us and Betty was close and otherwise amused, I left her off the lead. Betty then trotted up very slowly and in ultra-cute style to say hello. Two of the boys came to greet her, but the other was slightly more reticent. I enthused that she was just a puppy and was very friendly, but he kept his distance.

After getting a fuss from the first two boys, Betty approached the other boy, hoping for more of the same. The boy then suddenly took flight, running off in a farcical escape from this terrifying puppy. As Betty is a Border terrier, a group of dogs bred for chasing, this was the beginning of a nightmare. She set off at pace to catch up with this speedy stranger, barking with delight and ignoring my commands to come. The boy was heading straight for the open gate and the road outside, but luckily I am a regular jogger and managed to cut him off, yelling for him to stop. Betty then immediately stopped, looking up at the boy and me to see where the next game would come from.

With harsh words spoken and lead put on, I asked Betty to sit and gave her a treat before returning to work for a little lie down!

Lessons learned

Remain vigilant in parks. Friendly dogs can make us complacent when it comes to meeting people, so always chaperone any interaction to avoid frightening situations occurring for you, other people or your puppy.

Health reminders

Preventative treatments

Worming is again due this month, with most puppies now large enough to move on to tablet wormers. Flea-control application is important, especially at this stage when your puppy is venturing further afield outdoors. There are a number of 'all in one' treatments available now, either in topical or chew form, making it easy to treat your puppy regularly; just make sure that you weigh them frequently to ensure that the correct dose is given.

Health checks and routines

Continue to examine your puppy in general, so that any issues such as skin problems, parasites and eye and ear infections can be identified early on and treated or prevented. Grooming, teeth brushing and bathing are practical ways to give your dog a regular, all-over check. Keeping them familiar with these procedures at home will make it less stressful when you visit the vet.

Check your pup's ear canals for wax build-up and foreign bodies. Liquid cleaners can be obtained from your vet to keep your puppy's ears looking and smelling clean.

Your puppy's nails may have grown long enough to injure you or be pulled out, causing pain. Walking them on roughened surfaces such as cement footpaths is the best way to keep nails short. Check them regularly and if necessary trim or grind them or get them professionally manicured.

You may notice some teeth falling out, but don't worry: these are baby (deciduous) teeth and will be replaced by adult ones. Provide larger chews and toys, as your puppy's jaw is getting stronger and needs an increasingly vigorous workout.

Check your puppy's weight regularly both at home and at the vet's, giving larger portions of food as they develop to keep their growth on track. By four months of age the rate of weight gain will have slowed down in most smaller-breed dogs, while larger-breed dogs continue to grow at a considerable rate.

Check your puppy's collar to ensure that it isn't too tight after months of growing at a fast rate. Two fingers should fit comfortably under the collar to remain secure.

Weeks 20–24

GROWING PAINS

This stage will see the relationship between you and your puppy move from parent and child towards mutual companionship. Growing pains that herald sexual maturity, akin to those of a human teenager, will test that happy picture. A higher level of training and specialist disciplines can now be explored, to mould your puppy into the dog of your dreams.

Weeks 20–24: Owner checklists

What your puppy may do

- Overpower you with exuberance and brute strength
- Become increasingly destructive
- Show signs of sexual maturity

🐾 Have a renewed thirst for knowledge, game playing and training

If you are able to identify any of these in your dog, it shows that now is not the time for puppy complacency.

What you should do

🐾 Deal with the signs of sexual maturity with understanding and by seeking advice (which should never be cause for embarrassment)

🐾 Check out advanced training classes

🐾 Exercise your puppy more outdoors as they grow older and wiser

🐾 Discuss any behavioural concerns with professionals

At least two of these should be in hand.

Health reminders

🐾 Baby teeth will continue to be lost as adult teeth come through; brushing should begin in earnest

🐾 Monthly worming is again needed, plus flea treatments, depending on the preparation used

🐾 Continue with regular grooming and health checks

🐾 Monitor your puppy for changes associated with sexual maturity and consider neutering

Parental duties

Assess and adjust

Energetic, enthusiastic and bold, your much bigger puppy still has a great capacity to learn. Take stock of your puppy's development and correct any deficiencies now. With improved experience and confidence on and off the lead, walking your puppy becomes less of a job and more of a joy.

Your puppy's behaviour

Genetically predisposed behaviours

The breed of your puppy can again be used as an indicator of what behaviours to expect. A history of certain behavioural traits in the breed will encourage you to remain vigilant when setting them free within the confines of a 21st-century home and further afield.

Declaration of independence

Your puppy's new-found independence and free-thinking spirit will be appreciated when in the park, but may not be so welcome indoors, where mild destructiveness may become an all-out war on your belongings. Chewing and tearing of fixtures and furnishings awaits owners of untrained, unexercised or under-stimulated puppies. Trust to roam the whole home can only be given to the select few. Relaxation of confinement within your home can backfire for the over-eager owner keen to be free of crates and baby gates, with house-training taking a backward step and toileting accidents appearing in all manner of new places.

Big, bold and brash

Your puppy is a bigger, stronger and more self-aware animal at this stage, able to inflict serious damage or injury if previous training has been lacking. Jumping up, biting and barging are all forms of rough play that they may attempt to indulge in, with a few ill-prepared owners now regretting obtaining their, now less cute, canine housemate. Some smaller breeds will be nearing their adult size, while larger breeds still have a way to go.

Puppy puberty

Smaller breeds will be moving into adolescence, so be prepared for the hormonal rollercoaster that this prequel to sexual maturity can bring. Scent marking and aggression, particularly towards other male dogs, can be seen in young males, while insecurity, indifference and mood swings greet the owners of female adolescent puppies.

These behaviours can wax and wane with either sex for a period of up to three years, as newly adult dogs come to terms with their surging hormone levels. Older puppies will have sexual desires and capabilities that must be curbed, as their physical development and maturity levels are insufficient to deal with the consequences...if you know what I mean?!

What your puppy may do

Behaviour that needs understanding

With the onset of sexual maturity, the behaviour of some male puppies can become generally unruly. Lifting his leg indoors to scent mark, and becoming interested in female dogs, showing aggressive behaviour towards other males, roaming and selective deafness when outdoors are all consistent with male puppy growing pains. Female puppies during oestrus (heat) seem erratic and can become insecure, aggressive or subdued. They can also regress in house-training when they are in season, urinating and defecating indoors after months of not doing so.

Behaviour that needs managing

With healthy growth and development, your maturing puppy can begin to overpower you with exuberance and brute strength. Aggressive tendencies around food may develop and major damage to household items, as well as jumping onto furniture, visitors and you, can all occur if your energetic and confident puppy has not been suitably parented. Mood swings and hormonal surges are negative influences that can lead to a lack of concentration and renewed house soiling, working against the positives of your puppy's renewed thirst for knowledge, game playing and training.

What you should do

Dealing with sexual behaviours

Learning the signs of sexual maturity will help you to be prepared to deal with them when they inevitably arrive. Keep a close eye on your puppy's new-found interest in the opposite sex, which can lead to unwanted pregnancy or aggression if it is allowed to go unchecked.

Day-to-day discipline

Continue to give clear and fair direction to your developing puppy, who is still learning the ropes of living life alongside humans. Avoid over-excitement when people arrive at the door by passing through doors first, and never accept aggression. Consult an animal behaviourist if food aggression is experienced to avoid this worrying behaviour plaguing your puppy (and you) into adulthood.

Exercise and training

Start exercising with your puppy more as they near full-grown size, bearing in mind that they may have attained adult stature but have a way to go in the maturity stakes. Reconsider training classes if you are not already enrolled, or look into specialized training and activities for your puppy to keep them stimulated.

BETTY'S DIARY
Progress to a point

Day 106 *Pushing boundaries with your puppy can be fraught with failure. Any modification of training regimes and freedoms granted depends on your puppy's varying responses. Betty was no different during this phase, giving me much to be proud of, while occasionally necessitating apologies.*

With Betty changing from black to a patchy wheat colour and nearing full size, her mental maturity still had some way to go. Well versed in basic training and toilet training at home, Betty was a joy and loved by all who met her. With much socialization and habituation as a younger puppy, she was completely at ease with traffic, other dogs and the varied residents of our friendly locality. She would routinely come when called in the park, after consistent use of long leads and treats when on our own, but could not be trusted completely off the lead when the park was shared by others. She could not resist meeting other dogs in her happy, confident way, which rarely elicited ill will, and meeting children brought a whole new meaning to the word 'excited'.

As previously mentioned, it is hard to train friends and family to be good dog trainers, and verging on the impossible with children. Considering the speed with which Betty would rush to her child idols, it is understandable that this could result in fright. A jumping, flailing child is great entertainment for a perky puppy and Betty could never resist jumping up too – a scene I witnessed on Day 106. Thankfully, the parents of the frightened child were dog lovers and hoped their son would appreciate Betty's affections. I felt terrible that he had been upset, even though Betty was completely friendly and just wanted to greet him. With time, we coaxed a smile from the child and I held Betty safely so that she could gently lick his hand. After bidding the family farewell and walking home, I made a conscious decision to temper Betty's off-lead exploration while further improving her recall skills.

Lessons learned

Know your puppy, constantly assess your environment, modify your training plan if mistakes are made and have an apology at the ready if your puppy still manages to do the wrong thing.

Health reminders

Preventative treatments

The last of the monthly intestinal worming treatments is due, and then treatments every three months are recommended. Lungworm and heartworm must still be treated monthly, though some longer-acting products are available. Flea-control application may be due again; or, depending on the product used, it might be included in the monthly 'all in one' treatment prescribed by your vet.

Health checks and routines

Grooming and general health checks should be carried out on a regular basis. Adult teeth should be almost through, with a routine in place to keep them clean using daily brushing and chews to ensure good dental health. Ear plucking may be required to keep your puppy's ear canals clear.

Toys and chews

Be on the lookout for great new toys that will stimulate your maturing puppy and help keep them out of mischief. Increase the size of chews and toys to minimize the potential for choking.

Neutering

As hormones are racing at around this age, you should begin to consider the issue of neutering, which is generally carried out once your puppy has reached full maturity. Discuss the pros and cons with your vet.

PAWS FOR THOUGHT
Guilty or not guilty?

Many behaviourists believe that guilt is an emotion experienced only by higher primates such as humans. But owners often report their canines acting guiltily when they have perpetrated the unthinkable – for example, I have heard tales of owners finding an embarrassed-looking dog and then minutes later a chewed rug or a steaming pile of you-know-what in the kitchen. Canine body language is subtle and complex, used to diffuse a situation and avert aggression in wild and domestic dogs. This skill can be exhibited towards you when you find something askew after leaving puppy home alone and your rising frustration and tension levels are easily detected by your attuned canine companion. They are much better natural readers of body language than we are, so they may attempt to appease us with gestures that we incorrectly perceive as guilt.

Envy, guilt, spite and an ability to read their owners' minds are some of the complex skills that dog enthusiasts commonly claim to have found in their four-legged friends but that are scientifically harder to prove. What emotional complexities lie beneath the furry exterior of your dog's cranium? The jury is out...

Six months and beyond

THE ASPIRING ADULT

Having matured under your watchful ownership, your young dog will continue to develop physically and emotionally over the next few years. Further training, attention, play and exercise will forge your relationship into one that will last a lifetime.

Six months plus: Owner checklists

What your puppy may do

- 🐾 Reach full height (continuing to fill out until up to two years of age)
- 🐾 Show signs of sexual maturity and behaviour
- 🐾 Be newly fearful or shy of familiar objects and people

- Become increasingly dominant, territorial or protective
- Dislike or show outward aggression towards other dogs of the same sex

What you should do

- Increase training and exposure to new environments while avoiding fear-evoking situations
- Remain consistent and don't relax established codes of behaviour
- Check out new ways to interact with your young dog to build their confidence
- Congratulate yourself on raising your puppy and look forward to enjoying life together

Health reminders

- Worm and apply flea treatment based on your dog's weight, as recommended by your vet
- Consider neutering
- Reassess your dog's diet
- Plan to take your dog to the vet at least once a year (twice is better) for a general health check-up
- Groom and examine your dog regularly to pick up early warning signs of disease, and maintain dental hygiene with teeth brushing or dental chews
- Familiarize yourself with canine first aid, as well as the signs of illness in dogs

What to expect

Size and weight

Smaller breeds will have reached their full-grown height and weight, while larger-breed dogs continue growing until around eighteen months to two years of age. The rate of weight gain for larger-breed puppies will finally slow down from the massive gains of the last few months, already having markedly slowed in smaller breeds from around four months of age.

Behavioural and social development

Behaviour will vary greatly in your puppy depending on breed and the degree of training, socialization and habituation that they have received, with lessons continuing to be learned into adulthood. Sexual maturity will bring with it additional behavioural challenges. Using strong and confident leadership with kindness, patience and understanding, owners can help to alleviate and overcome these usually transient issues.

Your puppy's behaviour

Energy-driven

Whether your young dog is tenacious or rebellious, exuberant or over-excited, it is how you channel this energy that changes the way you perceive it. Begin to venture more deeply into the world of experiences and challenges that you can share with your dog, gradually increasing the difficulty of training. Also extend outdoor activities on a social level, allowing interactions with many other non-threatening dogs and humans.

Sexual maturity

Sexual behaviours will begin to surface at this stage of development, and can be addressed with patience, vigilance or neutering. Hormone surges can lead to some erratic behaviour, with certain individuals challenging humans in a bid to further assert themselves.

Fear revisited

Fearful tendencies can again be exhibited at this adolescent stage, and are commonly reported in young male dogs. Owner frustration and impatience at this sudden shyness are understandable, but reassuring your puppy rather than getting annoyed or angry at them is the only way to get through this awkward stage. Fear aggression can be expressed, and protectiveness of belongings or you may be new concerns to deal with.

Challenges ahead

Be mindful that your dog may be approaching adult size but has much to learn and experience before reaching emotional maturity. Be realistic with your expectations, appreciating that one foolish overestimation of your puppy's maturity and experience level can lead to physical and emotional scars that may never heal. Now that they have a full set of adult teeth, it can be disappointing to see a reoccurrence of chewing – a phase of territorial exploration that tends to pass quickly.

What your puppy may do

Physical changes

Your small-breed puppy may reach full height, while continuing to gain weight until one year. If your puppy is a larger breed, they are likely to continue to grow in height and weight up until two years of age. Their fur may also change, with the soft puppy coat being slowly replaced by a generally thicker adult coat.

In the case of an unlucky puppy, your vet may have already advised you of any unfortunate congenital (from birth) medical conditions they may suffer, which may begin to exhibit clinical signs as they reach full adult size and weight. An effective plan needs to be made to fully diagnose and treat these conditions as your puppy matures.

Behavioural changes

Your six-month-old dog may be newly fearful or shy of familiar objects and people. This is just something that can occur in puppies of this age, although most will be happily enjoying life in general. With sexual maturity, your puppy may begin, over the coming months, to become more assertive and test set boundaries. This needs to be quelled quickly. Showing new territorial or protective traits around the home and family, your young dog may dislike or display aggression towards other dogs of the same sex.

What you should do

Exercise and training

Focus on increased complexity of training and exposure to new environments, negotiated by you to avoid fear-evoking situations. Take a step back to assess your dog's progress, training yourself not to confront or coddle when they are nervous or fearful, but to be a calm and reassuring force instead. That said, remind yourself that you are the parent of a big puppy, not a fully grown dog; be as kind and emotionally supportive to them as you would be to teenage children moving into adulthood. Continue to investigate new ways to encourage your pup to interact with the world and its inhabitants if inherently nervous, in order to build confidence.

Day-to-day discipline

Continue to be a consistent, patient and fun puppy parent without relaxing established codes of behaviour. Take an overview of the situation and consider compiling a report card of their achievements and where they need more support. Appreciate where improvements can be made in family and park life and behaviour, and make them while you still have a youthful pup to mould. Be ready to halt any rough play or activity that may over-stimulate your maturing dog because this can lead to assertiveness or aggression, which can be frightening for some and take all your good work off track. Finally, congratulate yourself on raising your puppy into a healthy dog and look forward to a rewarding and happy life together.

Dealing with sexual behaviours

Remember that sexual maturity brings hormonally charged behavioural changes within your older puppy, particularly towards other dogs. Do your utmost to assess other dogs at a distance before allowing your dog to interact with them. If you have concerns regarding your dog's developing sexuality, discuss them with your vet while investigating the possibility of neutering in the coming months.

When to neuter

Canines should be allowed to gain full physical maturity prior to neutering, which is best gauged by sexual development. There are two schools of thought regarding spaying female dogs. One is to neuter before the first season, with each season proven to lead to an incremental rise in the development of mammary (breast) and other hormonally stimulated tumours later in life. The downside to pre-first-season neutering can be the development of hormonal urinary incontinence in rare cases, where the urinary sphincters do not develop properly without the stimulation of oestrogen, leading to weak bladders and urine leakage chiefly when sleeping.

If you decide to neuter a female dog after their first season, it is recommended that you wait at least a couple of months after signs of bleeding before booking them in for the procedure to reduce risk of internal haemorrhage. This allows for reproductive organs to reduce in size and blood-carrying capacity, making the procedure safer to perform with fewer complications. The standard minimum age for neutering dogs is six to nine months.

When it comes to neutering male dogs, there are a number of reasons why this makes sense. Firstly, to reduce overtly masculine traits such as male-to-male aggression or inappropriate sexual activity or behaviours. Secondly, it dramatically reduces the chance of your dog developing prostate problems (inflammatory enlargement or cancer) in later life. Finally, with high levels of testosterone, male dogs will constantly be on the lookout for a mate, leading to a canine companion who is sexually frustrated for life. As these behaviours are directly related to testosterone, removing the source (the testicles) by castration leads to a calmer and more relaxed dog who can happily live life with a human family without the need for romantic entanglements.

OLD WIVES' TAIL

A female dog should have one litter of puppies before she is spayed, as it is important for her to become fully developed.

No, this is not the case. If every owner of a female dog thought that, the world would be overrun with unwanted puppies! Spaying helps to keep unplanned pregnancies to a minimum, while decreasing the chances of your dog suffering mammary tumours later in life. Uterine infections and ovarian cancer are no longer a concern once your bitch is neutered; nor will she continue to go through the behavioural highs and lows associated with seasons. If your female dog doesn't have puppies, she will be the same dog as if she had had them – just without the potential health risks.

SKULLY'S DIARY
Skully is spayed

Day 165 *After deciding to wait until three months after Skully's first season to have her neutered, my wife nervously brought our beloved fur baby into the veterinary practice for the procedure. As vets, we take anaesthetics and surgery very seriously, though performing a spay on your own dog with your wife watching adds an understandable level of stress. With the procedure performed and our little fluffball waking up nicely, it reminded us both just how much we loved her after such a short time.*

Judging maturity

Differences between the breeds

Each breed matures differently, with the average dog reaching adult height at around nine months of age. Weight is determined by breed, diet and exercise, with a healthy larger dog continuing to gain muscle bulk until around 18 months of age. Adolescence is usually gauged by sexual maturity, which manifests itself in each sex differently. In females it is with the physical development of oestrus (heat): that is, when they come into season. Males change more behaviourally, with scent marking and aggression or nervousness towards other male dogs commonly seen.

Female sexual characteristics

- Swelling of vulva
- Bloody discharge for 5–7 days
- Mood swings, from overly affectionate to insecure, aggressive or subdued
- Hiding toys
- Apparent withdrawal from the pack or the family
- Increase or decrease in appetite
- Develops pica (appetite for strange foods, such as rocks, earth, etc.)

Male sexual characteristics

- Lifts leg to urinate, scent marking numerous trees and vertical objects in the neighbourhood and occasionally in the house
- Challenges owners
- Dislikes or fights other male dogs
- Overly excitable
- Shows attraction to female dogs

- Imitates sexual acts with furniture, stuffed toys, young children or the legs of adults
- Exhibits sexual arousal
- Generally unruly
- Roams if given the opportunity
- Fails to be attentive when outdoors
- Lack of appetite

Health reminders

Preventative treatments

Intestinal worming treatments are now given every three months. Flea treatment can be used consistently or during the warmer months in non-allergic dogs. Other parasitic treatments may be necessary depending on where you live. Familiarize yourself with local disease-carrying parasites and purchase preventatives to combat them.

Health checks and routines

Plan biannual visits to your vet for general health check-ups and to pick up conditions early, with yearly booster vaccinations recommended to continue to protect your dog against common diseases in their environment.

Routinely examine your dog when stroking them and after every walk, so that any changes in their condition or concerns about their health can be quickly addressed. Make sure you understand the signs of illness that a canine may exhibit (see page 214) so that your dog gets veterinary attention at an early stage when they need it most.

Grooming may need to be more regular during seasonal and maturity coat changes to deal with increased hair loss. You should continue to keep dental hygiene a priority, with daily teeth brushing or dental chews.

Feeding

Reassess your dog's nutritional requirements in consultation with your vet, checking to see if they are ready to graduate from puppy to adult foods.

Neutering

Neutering is normally recommended at the stage when your dog is fully grown in height and weight (see pages 158–9).

First aid

Find time to familiarize yourself with canine first-aid techniques so that you can aid your dog if they injure themselves when out and about or if other emergency situations occur where their wellbeing could be under threat (see pages 224–36).

BETTY'S DIARY
From puppy to dog

Days 135–8 *With the telltale signs of swollen vulva and reclusive behaviour, Betty became an adult by coming into season. Slightly off-colour for a day or two, she had a very small amount of bloody discharge and hid her toys under the sofa. Disappointingly, she suddenly began to urinate in the house again. Examination by her veterinarian father revealed a urine infection that required treatment. After a few days* the worst of the (still minimal) bleeding had resolved and toileting accidents in the house also improved with a course of antibiotics.

In terms of her behaviour, Betty suddenly graduated from occasional puppy misdemeanours to having a more mature, ladylike attitude, obeying house rules and following commands when outdoors with greater understanding and conviction. She was given a freer rein in her indoor pursuits as a reward for her new-found appreciation of living in a human world, which included asking to go outside to the toilet, eating well at allotted feeding times and relinquishing her love of chewing remote controls – all developments that were warmly welcomed. Result!

Lessons learned

Behavioural changes in your maturing puppy may be subtle and can indicate the onset of adulthood or illness, or both! Continue to challenge your developing puppy with greater freedoms indoors and extension of their socialization and experience outdoors. Appreciate how much patience has gone into getting your puppy to this stage and pat yourself on the back for a job well done.

Neutering

What it involves

Neutering is the surgical removal of the organs involved in reproduction – the testicles in males or the ovaries and uterus of females. This is the most common procedure performed by vets on pet dogs. It is a routine operation carried out under general anaesthetic.

The arguments for and against

Historically, neutering has been used to decrease unwanted pregnancy in females and control male aggression or arousal. Many recent studies have proven a distinct health advantage in neutering canines of both sexes at a young age, with a decrease in the incidence of malignant-tumour development later in life. Some owners (particularly men) can feel that castrating a male dog is taking away his life force, yet an unneutered pet male dog lives his whole life sexually frustrated in forced celibacy. Female dogs are prone to uterine infections (pyometra) later in life, which are prevented with the removal of the uterus if the dog is spayed as a youngster.

Many owners wish to have one litter of puppies prior to having their bitch spayed, yet aren't fully aware of the potential complications that can await their beloved female canine, such as the death of puppies, stillborn puppies, the death of the mother, post-parturition uterine infections or poor mothering leading to the owner needing to feed the puppies every two hours with supplementary food. Puppies can be a real joy when they are healthy and well looked after by their canine mum, but be mindful that your puppies may be purchased at the expense of rescue dogs in the community that desperately need homes.

Your dog is prone to weight gain post-neutering, but strict monitoring of exercise and nutrition can avoid this potential side effect. I recommend neutering for all animals that will not be used for breeding and for those suffering congenital disease or exhibiting hormonal-related behavioural problems. Every pet of mine has been neutered in the past without complication. There are strong arguments and emotive views on both sides to neuter or not to neuter, so it comes down to personal choice, along with your dog's individuality firmly in mind. This decision should only be made after thorough consultation with your vet.

Pros of neutering males

- Decreases aggressive tendencies
- Decreases crazed behaviour when a local bitch is in season
- Controls hypersexuality
- Reduces prevalence of prostatic disease and cancer
- Eliminates risk of testicular cancer
- Helps to resolve unwanted 'mounting' behaviour
- Dog becomes calmer and more obedient

Pros of neutering females

- Avoids unwanted puppies
- Decreases risk of mammary tumours
- Decreases risk of sexually transmitted disease
- Eliminates risk of ovarian cancer and uterine infections (pyometra)
- Eliminates seasons/bleeding
- Avoids the mood swings that tend to occur with hormonal surges

Cons of neutering

- Unable to parent puppies
- Can lose instinct needed for hunting
- Risk of general-anaesthetic and post-op complications
- Risk of weight gain
- A few immature females can develop hormonal-related incontinence later in life
- Behavioural changes may not suit certain canine professions, such as guard dogs

PUPPY REPORT CARD

At around six months, your dog should be able to perform the following activities. Answer this questionnaire honestly and seek out advice within this book and further afield if you've yet to gain top marks.

1	Sitting on command?	
2	Lying down when asked?	
3	Stay?	
4	Drop/Leave?	
5	Reduction in mouthing/biting? Some bull breeds may show more mouthing behaviours than some other breeds, and for longer.	
6	Come? Recall should be good and puppy should return to you if small distractions are present. Bigger distractions such as the presence of other dogs might still be challenging for a happy, sociable and energetic older puppy. Breeds such as sighthounds, scent hounds and huskies/akitas will likely need more intensive training in recall compared to other breeds.	
7	House-trained? Breeds such as pugs and dachshunds take longer to nail this.	
8	Jumping up? This should at least be reducing at this stage; if it's getting worse, this needs attention.	
9	Happy to be left alone for up to three hours? If not, work on building their resilience.	
10	Comfortable both at home and out and about, both socially and in different environments? If not, build up their experiences, working with them so that they become a well-adjusted canine companion in all environments and in any company, either human or animal.	

If your adolescent pooch has not passed with flying colours, please don't lament – just complete this section to help you feel better!

1	Were you a less than perfect human as a teenager?	
2	Is your dog happy when you are around?	
3	Does your puppy love you?	
4	Do you love your puppy?	
5	Are you overall enjoying the puppy-parenting experience?	

If you answer yes to all of these, everything is just fine. Life is a journey, and every day is a school day for both us and our canine companions. Dogs are individuals and they learn at different speeds. Breed traits and genetics play a large role in your dog's behaviours, so the fact that they aren't doing something by six months of age does not necessarily mean you or they are doing anything wrong.

Just remember that no human or dog is perfect. Owning a puppy should be enjoyable overall (moments of exasperation and annoyance from both parties is OK!) There is always time to address issues if they are still present or arise during your long and loving life together.

Problem puppy

COPING WITH BAD BEHAVIOUR

Puppies can be expected to exhibit all manner of behaviours, some of which their owners will find undesirable. Understanding why these unwanted behaviours occur can help to prevent them becoming a lifelong problem, and addressing the early warning signs immediately will avoid the need to implement cures in the future.

Mouthing and aggression

A degree of **mouthing and mock-aggressive** playful behaviour is to be expected in a young, confident puppy finding their feet, and very rarely will they bite to cause actual harm. But biting or aggression in adult dogs can have **serious ramifications** for both you and your dog, so must be dealt with swiftly in your puppy through **training and socialization**.

Why

Play

Biting and mouthing littermates is the only play behaviour your puppy knows before arriving at your home. Mouthing is also key to exploring the world around them, using the high concentration of neurons around their gums to feel out their new world. When interacting with you they may continue this behaviour, mouthing your hands and feet in the same way they did with siblings to initiate a game. This behaviour is particularly undesirable when delicate-skinned children or elderly people are present, especially considering how sharp a young puppy's teeth can be. If allowed to continue, this type of playful mouthing can lead to injury and occasionally the development of aggressive tendencies in extreme cases. Chasing feet or clothing as you walk past is great fun and can also stimulate a puppy to play bite. This inappropriate behaviour must also be quickly quelled to avoid injury or damage.

Fear

This is the most common reason for a puppy to intentionally bite strangers. A puppy will rarely bite out of fear when young, preferring to hide behind their owner or rapidly remove themselves from a frightening situation. But as they grow older and more confident, your puppy may start to use biting to defend themselves in situations from which they cannot escape. Once a puppy begins biting, they can realize how effectively it can be used to get out of an unpleasant experience, and may begin resorting to it as a first line of defence towards other dogs and strange people.

Excitement

Puppies will mouth mostly when they are excited. Be mindful that children will likely create excitement and when they squeal or run away, it is seen by your puppy as part of the game.

Miscommunication

Dogs have many ways of showing that they are angry or fearful without resorting to biting. Vocalizations such as barking or growling and body language such as pinned-back ears, bared teeth and erect fur are used by dogs to avoid conflict. Many new owners are not well versed in canine body language and an inexperienced puppy may not be sufficiently familiar with the body language displayed by other dogs, so any actual physical aggression that takes place can often be blamed on miscommunication.

Resource/food-related aggression

Some puppies will feel the need to guard their food and this can become a serious issue, especially when there are young children residing in the same household. This sort of aggression is seen more commonly in puppies that have suffered from lack of food in the past. It can be considered a reversion to wild-dog behaviour, when individuals needed to protect their food from others in the pack.

Tiredness

Just like us, puppies can get a little grumpy when they are tired. Mouthing can be worse when your puppy has not had enough rest, so make sure they are getting sufficient sleep in a low-traffic area, and consider timeouts in crates or controlled areas to enforce some downtime.

Prevention

Predictability

Learn the basics of canine body language (see page 75), as being able to read adeptly the signs that your puppy uses to communicate their feelings will avoid aggressive tendencies becoming the norm. At an early age, your puppy will bite only when playing, so always have toys at the ready to substitute for your hand.

If your puppy is a keen biter of skirts or trouser legs (or the feet under them) as they swish past, try to wear them as little as possible, or keep puppy secure in a playpen in a high-traffic area of your home so they get used to them without being able to react. When your puppy begins going outside, they may be fearful of other dogs and people. Never force an interaction or meeting that may stimulate fear, protecting your puppy at all times from frightening situations to avoid aggression.

Socialization and habituation

Ensuring that your puppy is well socialized with other people and dogs (once he has been fully vaccinated), and exposing them to many potentially frightening places and objects in a calm and relaxed way are the best techniques to avoid fear-related aggression (see pages 84–5). Be careful to avoid reinforcement of nervousness through coddling your puppy, instead offering reassurance and guidance while keeping all of their four paws on the floor and at a safe distance. This gives your puppy the ability to shrug off initial fears and gain confidence through experience.

Avoid force

It is important always to bear in mind that treating aggression with aggression simply will not work. If anything, shouting or using force will escalate the situation further or result in your puppy learning to use aggression more readily next time. Remember that fear is at the root of most of the aggressive behaviours in your puppy, so you should try to avoid physical punishment at all costs and instead search for a considered solution.

Training

A well-trained dog is a well-adjusted dog that will respond to your every command (see page 108). Once you have identified a potentially dangerous situation, it means that you will be able to extricate your puppy from harm before any aggression manifests itself.

Cure

Avoid rough play

Discouraging children and adults from engaging in rough play with your puppy will reduce over-excitement and then mouthing. Children playing inappropriately with your puppy can cause this potentially dangerous behaviour to continue for longer. Teach children how to play with puppy using toys or, even better, show them how to calmly train puppy in order to keep activity sessions positive and safe.

Play with toys

By using appropriate substitutes for arms and clothing in mouthing, your puppy will eventually learn what is acceptable to mouth and what isn't. Shake toys to stimulate play or use toys that squeak to keep your puppy's interest on the toy and not on your hand. Be patient, as biting is a lesson that needs to be unlearned from your puppy's time with his siblings, and playing with toys initially seems far less fun to them than playing rough games with you. Channelling their energy into a different activity is also helpful, and snuffle mats (where puppy searches for food between rubber fingers), Kongs, puzzle feeders and scatter feeding are all great ways to encourage puppy to use their nose rather than their teeth.

Tell puppy it hurts

If your puppy is consistently mouthing during play, loudly say 'ouch' while standing up and ignoring them. This will momentarily halt their mouthing, teaching them that aggression towards you will result in the end of play. If puppy leans towards you with mouth open during play, quietly command 'no' and reward them with affection if they stop. Even if a biting incident is deemed accidental, you should halt the game immediately so that puppy quickly learns that teeth are not allowed.

Time out

Keeping a collar on your puppy and a lead in your pocket at all times indoors is handy for separating a puppy from excitable children or leading them away from a potentially dangerous situation. When indoors, if a play session results in your puppy biting you, say 'no', then leave them and walk into another room (one with a baby gate to avoid them following is best) to calm the situation down for a few minutes – the puppy should then make the connection between biting/aggression and being separated from you.

Reward positive behaviour

Train your puppy to overcome their fears by rewarding calm behaviour. When a previously feared stimulus such as another dog or a stranger is at a safe distance to avoid provoking a fearful response, reward your puppy for being relaxed by initiating a game or feeding them a treat (diversion and counter-conditioning). Repeat the process with patience and caution, bringing either your puppy closer to the stimulus or vice versa until they are acting calmly without any aggression.

Give and take – food or resource guarding

A puppy who guards their food bowl when you come near it believes that you are going to take their food away. Firstly, train all family members never to take food or treats away from your puppy if they growl when someone approaches their food bowl, and to avoid escalating any aggression by never shouting at them. Train your puppy to welcome your approach to their food bowl by bringing something even more tasty than they are already consuming. Once puppy is ready to allow your approach, begin to lift the bowl out of their reach mid-meal, placing a few treats in their bowl before replacing it. If your puppy has hold of something potentially dangerous, the minimum amount of force should be used to remove the offending item and you should offer a more attractive alternative to encourage them to drop it in favour of a tasty treat, to end the situation positively.

Animal behaviourists

Animal behaviourists delve into the cause, function, development and evolution of behaviour in animals and relate this knowledge to the treatment of behavioural problems in pets and wild animals. Given that behavioural issues in companion animals are quite complex, qualified behaviourists and counsellors are recommended by veterinarians to help distraught owners deal with their problem pets.

Consulting an animal behaviourist is advisable if your puppy seems to be developing worrying behaviours, such as biting, which you are unable to halt or control. Your vet will be able to advise you only so far, because without seeing how you interact with your puppy on walks and in your home environment, they won't have access to all the information needed to solve the problem. An animal behaviourist will visit your home, observe your puppy, discuss the issue at length and devise appropriate and practical solutions.

Always gain the services of a specialist animal behaviourist through your veterinarian by referral, as this will enable you to locate the most experienced and qualified practitioners in your area to help solve your puppy's problem. Working side by side with a behaviourist, your vet must be consulted in case any medical conditions are causing the issues or medications are needed to treat the problem effectively.

Over-excitement

Every dog owner wants their puppy to greet visitors enthusiastically and **without fear**. As many visitors will also be pleased to meet them, the combination can result in a puppy that **constantly jumps up** when meeting **new people** or in exciting situations. Endearing in a small puppy, this behaviour can become a **real nuisance** in an older, **heavier dog**, leading to complaints about **muddy pawprints, ruined clothing, scratches or bruises.**

Why

Canine greetings

Face-to-face greetings are a natural way for two dogs to meet. As humans are bipedal (we stand on two legs), your face is far removed from your puppy's – resulting in them wanting to get closer to it by jumping up to say hello.

Attention seeking

A puppy will quickly learn that jumping up at people gains a response, either positive or negative. In the early days, your puppy will cause little damage or injury indoors, so the behaviour cycle of jumping up followed by attention is allowed to continue.

Bad table manners

As dogs are natural scavengers, your puppy will quickly appreciate that when you or your family sit down to the table, tasty titbits will follow.

Puppy will learn that these morsels come from the table and may begin to jump up to get closer to the food supply in order to help themselves.

Untrained others

As a general rule, this behaviour is not performed with members of the family who are well versed in dog training. However, other people whom the puppy meets will often encourage or allow them to jump up, making it very difficult to reinforce the lesson that it is not an acceptable way for them to behave. Also, many people are not dog lovers and they may find it off-putting if your puppy jumps up to greet them.

Prevention

Greet puppy at their level

Crouch down to their level immediately on your arrival home or whenever you are giving puppy attention, so that you don't encourage jumping up in the first place. Teach visitors to react similarly when your puppy approaches them.

Restrain

Use a lead on your puppy both indoors and out or hold them when meeting people, especially children, so that they do not automatically jump up at them as a standard greeting.

No table treating

Teach all the family and your friends not to treat the dog when they are sitting at the dining table so that puppy doesn't expect to get any food treats when you sit down to eat.

Basic training

Training your puppy to return to you as soon as they are called (see page 108) will help to prevent them from making contact with fellow park-goers who are not so keen on dogs or who are unaware of how to interact with an excitable puppy. Once puppy is securely on their lead, you can decide whether the interaction is a good idea or not. When allowing your puppy to meet people, use the lead or a hand on their collar to prevent them from jumping up.

Cure

Ignorance is bliss

Make it a rule not to give your puppy any attention until all of their four feet are on the ground. Boredom is a powerful tool to use in disciplining your puppy. Ignoring them will ensure your puppy will quickly lose interest in you, stop jumping up and walk off. As soon as they calm down, command them to come to you and sit, then crouch down to give the attention deserved for good behaviour. It is almost impossible to use this technique when your large-breed puppy has grown and still jumps up, so use it consistently and robustly while you still can.

Teach others how to react

Giving visitors to your home a quick lesson in how to react when your puppy jumps up is paramount in training them not to do so. Children in particular need guidance, as their excitable natures tend to incite your puppy to jump up at them. Teach visitors to stand up straight, with arms folded and looking away from the puppy. Tell them to ignore the puppy, and, when puppy has all four paws on the ground, reinforce the behaviour by saying 'good' calmly (saying it excitedly may cause the puppy to jump up again).

When the correct behaviours are performed, visitors should crouch down to give the puppy praise and treats. If the puppy again lunges playfully for the face, tell your visitors to retreat and halt all contact until puppy is again still. Consider recruiting understanding friends and family for the training process, repeating the exercise as many times as possible.

Avoid physical or verbal punishment

Pushing your puppy away or verbally reprimanding them harshly can be interpreted by them as an encouragement to play rough in the same way. This may worsen the situation, occasionally leading to a further escalation of playful or aggressive responses in your maturing puppy (see page 136).

Mounting

An extension of jumping up that has sexual overtones, mounting can be regarded by owners as anything from horrifying to amusing. Trying to mount another puppy or a person is fairly **normal canine behaviour that in most cases is not sexual in nature.** The behaviour is observable in **male and female puppies from a few months of age into sexual maturity and beyond.**

Why

Play

In young puppies, mounting tends to be a playful behaviour between individuals, when they jump on top of each other and roll around in half-hearted fighting. Excessive play with owners or upon the arrival of visitors can stimulate this behaviour, which your puppy enacts to release anxiety and tension.

Dominance display

In wild dogs, mounting a member of the pack is a clear statement of dominance and higher ranking. This ranking gives rights to females and other resources coveted by the pack. In domestic dogs, a puppy may constantly mount as a sign of insecurity, stress or over-excitement.

Sexual contact

During puberty, a male dog can be seen to mount other dogs and people in response to surging testosterone levels.

Prevention

Neutering

If you think the mounting is sexual or occurring as your puppy reaches puberty, ask your vet about neutering (see pages 164–5). Around one-third of castrated males show immediate improvement due to decreased testosterone. Female dogs seen mounting during heat also routinely show improvement after being spayed.

Cure

Increase exercise intensity

Burn off your puppy's excess energy, which can lead to mounting, by exercising them more vigorously. Increased training and the use of enrichment toys such as Kongs and puzzles can also direct mental energy in a more positive way.

Keep puppy calm

Remove puppy from living areas until visitors have sat down, then allow them to join you and keep their attention with treats.

Don't shake your leg

This will heighten the reward gained by a mounting puppy. Advise visitors to keep their leg still while detaching the puppy without giving them undue attention. Call puppy away and reward them for doing complying.

Do nothing

With consistent training, exercise and maturity, your puppy will hopefully grow out of this behaviour in time. Patience, tolerance and time will pay dividends.

WOOF!

Excessive vocalization

Barking is a **normal vocalization** made by dogs (except of course the barkless Basenji) to **communicate** with each other and guard their environment. After aggression, **excessive vocalization** is the next most likely cause of **complaint** to be levelled at your dog and you. A problem regularly facing the owners of fast-reacting, edgy canines such as **terriers**, this nuisance behaviour is more common in **smaller-breed dogs**.

Why

Attention seeking

This is the most common cause of excessive barking in your young puppy. After leaving the comfort of mum and siblings, vocalization is one way your puppy can learn to get your attention. This is not a natural behaviour, as in the wild it would be likely to draw unwanted attention from predators.

Guarding territory

One of the reasons that dogs were first invited into human homes was as a guard, warning their owners of an intruder with successive barks. This trait was then selectively bred to improve their guarding abilities, resulting in certain breeds being particularly vocal.

Boredom or frustration

Being bored or left on their own can trigger a dog to bark in an attempt to be reunited with you and your family. This may begin as occasional barking, but can graduate to bouts of howling.

Fear or anxiety

Any perceived threat may stimulate your puppy to bark as a way to ward off danger or alert the rest of the pack. Usually reserved for unfamiliar people or objects, these high-pitched barks tend to make your puppy feel better, thus encouraging them to continue barking.

Prevention

Exercise

A tired dog is a quiet dog. Boredom, frustration and excess energy can all lead to a more vocal pooch who is constantly on high alert in their environment rather than resting calmly. Giving sufficient physical and mental exercise, with basic training, long walks (based on breed, age and health, of course) and play with toys and balls are all key to dialling down the barks.

Isolate and reduce the stimulus

Your dog barks because they are stimulated to do so, so understanding and eliminating these motivators wherever possible is important for a calm home environment. Excluding your pooch from certain rooms, keeping them away from doors, bringing them inside from the yard when barking or using opaque film to reduce your canine's ability to see clearly out of low-level windows are big blunt first steps towards reducing excessive vocalization. If your dog barks when the doorbell goes, then ask people to call ahead instead; if your dog barks at other dogs, choose a time to visit the park when fewer people are around. Anything that can reduce your dog's reactivity and need to bark is a positive step forward.

Intervention

If you can see your dog is about to bark, intervene before they do so. There are a number of pre-bark cues that dogs may exhibit, including erect ears, standing to attention, rushing to the door or boundary fence, or even mild growls or grunts, which if noted and quickly responded to with the invitation of play or a treat may see off any barking. The use of a long lead can help with this when training your puppy outdoors, giving them the freedom to react normally but still allowing you to gain control ahead of any barking outbursts.

Ignorance is bliss

You *must* ignore your puppy when they are barking for attention, or they will quickly learn that you will come whenever called...or barked at! As you would ignore a child throwing a tantrum, give attention to your puppy only when they are quiet and well behaved. Ignoring your puppy is hard ,for sure, but do try not to yell at, look at or touch your barking pup, all of which can be misinterpreted by them as a reward for the behaviour you are trying to stop. Turn away from the barking when it occurs, waiting for the moment they are quiet to reward them with a treat, whether it be food or praise. Once your dog clicks that being quiet means attention or food, build up the time that they must remain quiet for and continue to make it worth their while with positive things and experiences.

Don't encourage them

A barking young puppy can be very cute, but giving them attention for it is a recipe for disaster. Never encourage your pup to bark, as this will be the first method they choose to express themselves as they mature, resulting in an overly vocal dog.

Socialization

The more socialized a puppy is, the less they fear, which means the less they feel the need to bark. Avoiding potentially frightening situations also helps to avoid excessive vocalization becoming the norm.

Environmental enrichment

Provide lots of toys and treats throughout the day at varying times so that your puppy never feels neglected or bored. Training is a good opportunity to allow your dog to communicate with you in non-verbal ways.

COMMON QUESTIONS
Barking

My puppy is driving me crazy with their incessant barking. I have tried everything to stop them. Should I use one of those shock barking collars as a last resort?

Do *not* use collars that give your puppy an electric shock each time they bark – these are cruel and don't address the cause of barking in the first place. If barking is a major concern, seek the professional advice of an animal behaviourist (see page 176), who will be able to help you tackle the problem without resorting to physical torture.

Cure

Reward quietness

Rewarding your puppy when they are silent around previously bark-stimulating or frightening things is a difficult technique to master, as it requires attentiveness and quick thinking. Barking can be quite tiring for your puppy and using this approach will soon teach them that being quiet is a much more successful and less labour-intensive strategy.

Desensitization

A commonly used term in canine behaviour, desensitization is a technique of exposing a dog to a stimulus that would normally lead to an undesirable response – in this case barking – at such low levels to the point that there is no response...you guessed it: no barking. Once you have isolated what causes your dog to bark, move them as far away as possible from that particular stimulus (whether it is another dog or a jogger) so that they no longer bark when they see it. Using lots of tasty treats and even asking a fellow dog owner to help, treat your dog when the stimulus moves into vision but your dog is quiet, and stop attention and treats when the stimulus moves out. This will, over many days and weeks of repeated training periods, lead to counter-conditioning: basically, you will have a dog whose brain has been rewired into seeing their specific bark stimulus as something that leads to a treat rather than vocalizing. As your dog becomes less bark reactive, gradually increase the proximity of the stimulus, challenging them to remain quiet and calm as you reward them with treats, games and fuss.

Reduction

A dog can't bark when they have something in their mouth – fact – and will likely do so much less barking when lying down in a bed away from the action. If your dog barks when people knock on the door, for example, then ask your dog to go to their bed and offer them a chew or toy to keep them happy and engaged while your visitors are welcomed into the house. Training your dog to go to their bed when visitors arrive means they are less likely to feel any level of fear, protectiveness or anxiety when strangers enter the house and this should reduce the frequency of barking. With time and patience, many pet parents will begin to notice their obliging pooch actively heading to their bed when the doorbell goes. This, my friends, is the sign that you really have cracked the barking business.

Chewing

Chewing is a normal and natural behaviour and should be expected throughout your puppy's life, even well into adulthood. Gaining a good understanding of chewing while your puppy is young should help you avoid home devastation when they get older...and stronger!

Why

Wild tendencies

After wild dogs have caught and killed their prey, they are faced with the hard task of devouring it. This requires patient chewing of the carcass, tearing at the skin, bones and sinews. Your puppy will exhibit this genetically inherited behaviour when chewing in your home – for instance, when they hold down a ball and attempt to tear off its exterior in the same way that a wild dog would deal with captured prey.

Breed

Some specific breeds of dog, such as gundogs, have been trained for many years to fetch hunted game. Using their mouths from an early age is therefore an integral part of their growth and learning process.

Teething

Like human babies, puppies go through a teething process. In dogs this usually occurs from three to six months of age, with most breeds having adult teeth by six to seven months. Chewing can help to alleviate some of the discomfort of teething, as well as encouraging the baby (deciduous) teeth to fall out and stimulating the growth of the adult teeth.

Exploration

Because they have a high concentration of nerve receptors along the gum line, puppies benefit from exploring different aspects of objects, such as texture and consistency, through chewing. Investigation of their environment in this way can continue until adulthood, which in large-breed dogs extends to around 18 months of age.

Prevention

Vigilance

There's a simple rule when your puppy is very young: don't trust them! You should puppy-proof your home thoroughly by keeping all chewable or valuable items off the floor, lifting electrical wires out of reach and putting shoes in cupboards (see page 44). Consider buying a playpen when you can't constantly watch your puppy to keep them enclosed in a safe area, and fill it only with their own things that are you don't mind being destroyed (see page 88). Shoes and wicker baskets are real chewing favourites, so if you want them to remain intact, keep them out of puppy's reach.

Toys

These should be carefully chosen to ensure they have a different texture to everyday objects in the home. Rubber toys are ideal, as a dog cannot mistake them for cloth or wood. These toys can be made more appealing by placing flavoured pastes or treats inside them, which will keep your puppy entertained for hours. Snuffle toys, Kongs and food puzzles are all readily available online and can save your possessions from being nibbled. Always remember to check toys and replace them if they become damaged, as parts can dislodge and could injure your puppy or be swallowed.

Chews

Both rawhide and commercially made chews will give your puppy the opportunity to satiate their need to chew on a tasty morsel, while cleaning their teeth and stimulating their gums at the same time. Only give your puppy chews when you are around, so that you are on hand in case they have any difficulties. You should also be sure to use them sparingly, as many chews are high in fat and can lead to dogs developing weight problems.

Cure

Caught in the act

Don't verbally reprimand a puppy when you catch them in the act of chewing, as you will make them wary of you and this may lead to your puppy targeting the same object but out of your sight. It is best that your puppy feels confident enough to chew in front of you so that you are able to control what they have access to and avoid destruction of precious belongings. Instead, offer up something appropriate to chew, such as a toy, either by instigating a game or including a tasty treat, rewarding them with praise at the same time.

Deterrents

Effective deterrents in the form of bitter sprays are readily available from pet stores and are a harmless way of protecting larger items from your puppy's over-active jaws. Spraying is a particularly good strategy for objects that can't be hidden away from your puppy, such as table legs or sofa cushions. However, the sprays may stain so make sure you test them first on a small area of the object to be treated.

Mix it up

Change the range of toys and chews available to your puppy so that boredom doesn't set in and lead them astray. You can build up a stock of toys with different shapes and consistencies and rotate them on a weekly basis.

Don't give in

Just because your puppy has destroyed an off-limits object doesn't mean that you should then allow them to have the ruined item as a chew plaything – for example, a pair of chewed-up shoes. This will confuse your puppy, as there will be no clear boundary between what they are allowed to chew and what they aren't. Take destroyed articles away calmly and encourage your puppy to play only with their own toys. Don't become complacent as your puppy grows, because with age come stronger jaws and an ability to cause greater damage.

BETTY'S DIARY
List of carnage

During the first six months of her life, Betty managed to chew her way through the following off-limits items:

- 🐾 *1 wallet full of cash and credit cards*
- 🐾 *1 pair of swimming goggles*
- 🐾 *1 standing wooden mask*
- 🐾 *numerous odd socks, which later reappeared with large holes*
- 🐾 *2 remote controls*
- 🐾 *1 personal cheque*
- 🐾 *selection of garden plants*
- 🐾 *2 telephone directories*
- 🐾 *1 work shoe*
- 🐾 *1 shirt off the clothesline (hours before I needed it to go on television!)*
- 🐾 *loads of bark removed from the garden and strewn around the house*
- 🐾 *2 DVDs*

Lessons learned

If you don't want any household or personal item chewed, keep it out of reach of your puppy and provide suitable chewable alternatives. Looking on the positive side, I have never kept my home so tidy than when the dogs were puppies!

Reinforcement and extinction

Sounding a little dramatic, this is the process of positively training a puppy to perform certain behaviours and have them almost forgetting to perform others that are less desirable. Certain behaviours become learned and reinforced behaviours will become practised. If certain undesirable behaviours are not reinforced and therefore not practised, these behaviours become extinct. Here are two examples:

If a puppy is jumping up at the coffee table for food, manage the environment so food is not left within reach. Set your puppy up for success, not failure, and then begin teaching them to leave. Your puppy will then learn 'leave' as an alternative behaviour for when they are around a table with food on it.

If we ignore jumping up we are not reinforcing it. Instead, reinforce 'sit' as an alternative behaviour. Jumping up will then become extinct as it is not being reinforced and is replaced by the far more desirable 'sit'.

House soiling

Urination and defecation in the home despite all efforts to house-train is a common reason for frustrated owners to consider re-homing their puppy. Remember that your puppy is likely to continue making the occasional toileting mistake up to six months of age and beyond, and recognize that certain factors out of their control – such as ill health or a change of routine – can lead to a backward training step.

Why

Lack of patience

Owners often do not show enough patience with their young charges when it comes to toilet training, resulting in a puppy that is frightened to toilet anywhere near their owner and 'accidents' that are found out of sight all over the home.

Incomplete toilet training

When a puppy finally takes themselves outdoors to urinate, owners are frequently so overwhelmed with relief that they stop actively toilet training beyond that moment. Others will keep a dog kennelled outdoors or left in the garden for an hour or two without giving appropriate instruction or reward for going in the right place. This can result in a dog that, if unable to go outside, will go indoors without concern.

Delayed punishment

Scolding your puppy for going to the toilet indoors after the event is pointless and can potentially make the situation worse. Your puppy will not be able to relate the verbal punishment with the earlier misdemeanour of going in the wrong place. This can result in a more fearful puppy that will shy away from you and toilet in more obscure places to escape your glare. You need to summon all your patience to clean up quietly and calmly without giving your puppy cause for concern.

Failure to teach bladder/bowel control

Many owners will continue to leave puppy training pads around the house for the times when they go out, preventing their puppy from learning bladder and bowel control. If you do the same, even the slightest filling of the bladder or bowels will prompt your puppy to go on their pad. Instead, you should encourage puppy to extend their capacity for bladder and bowel control in order to fit in with your need to leave the house for longer periods.

Once you have reached the milestone of your puppy toileting outside, continue to reinforce this action positively while removing training pads and increasing the amount of time your puppy must wait to go out. You may suffer a period of regression, but be patient and eventually your puppy will get the message.

Medical conditions

There are a number of medical conditions that can cause a puppy to suffer an inability to learn house-training. Take your puppy to be examined by your vet to ensure that the toileting problems endured are not associated with any illness or physical abnormality. A urine and/or faecal sample may prove useful.

Change in routine

Simply staying at work longer or asking friends to look after your, previously well-house-trained, puppy can result in a regression into toileting accidents. These are to be expected and some changes in routine need to occur so that your puppy can learn from their mistakes.

Prevention

Train your puppy

You can follow the house-training procedures outlined on pages 70–3 and 119 to establish the basis for a reliably house-trained puppy from the outset. You should be taking your puppy outside to toilet from their very first day at home.

Cure

Revamp your regime

Completely overhaul your routine at home with regimented feeding times for your puppy and regular-as-clockwork access to outdoors. Set an alarm hourly to actively take them outdoors, giving your puppy the opportunity to go in the right place. If they are soiling overnight, then night-time alarms are also necessary. You will have to fully commit to the time and effort this involves. Be extra lavish with your praise whenever your puppy goes to the toilet in the right place, taking treats with you on every trip outdoors to get the message across.

Stop all punishment

Previous over-punishment must be replaced with calm, rational behaviour on your part. Find different, positive ways to channel your anger, such as in a vigorous form of exercise. It is now recommended to avoid interrupting your pup if they are 'mid-flow' unless they are very close to the exit point, because they will have tended to empty their bladder enough that the urgency to go has waned. Interrupting may also lead to them finding more obscure places to toilet away from your prying eyes, meaning it will then be impossible to train them out of it. Instead, it's so much better to read the physical signs of needing to go in advance of them toileting and then get ahead of it by offering them the chance to go outside.

Signpost with urine

Wipe the cloth that you have used to clean up urine indoors over a position outdoors where you would like your puppy to go, such as in a corner of your garden or near a tree in your local park. The scent of their urine should help stimulate your puppy's desire to urinate near the chosen spot, which hopefully should herald a switch to a more consistent pattern of toileting outdoors.

Grass marks the spot

Unlike many surfaces in your home, grass has a texture that is unique. Therefore, your puppy will be able to determine that grass is different from anything that they might find indoors (such as carpet). The unique texture of grass enables you to give your puppy a clear indication that it is acceptable for them to toilet there.

Clean up wisely

With their ultra-sensitive nose, your puppy will be able to pick up their individual scent in areas where they have previously toileted, even after the offending material has been removed. Major cleaning must be undertaken to remove not only the urine or faeces, but also the scent. Many home-cleaning products simply mask odours, so hot biological washing solutions or odour eliminators need to be used to avoid your puppy from toileting in the same spot. Filling cracks in flooring and sealing grouting with waterproof material can also help to avoid stimulating scent from accumulating, while keeping your home clean and hygienic.

Nervousness and fear

Being ill at ease around strangers, **hanging back** from meeting visitors and **hiding** behind their owner at the slightest **traffic noise** are not behavioural traits of a puppy that will grow to appreciate all that the world has to offer. Although some dogs are born more **nervous** than others, you as an **understanding puppy parent** can draw upon the **strength of character** in your puppy to ensure a **carefree life** together.

Why

Genetic predisposition

Certain breeds of dog are known to be more nervous than others. German shepherd dogs, pointers and fox terriers, for example, are breeds that can suffer from nervous dispositions, although this can be overcome with understanding ownership from an early age. Puppies born to mothers that have suffered with stress during pregnancy are more likely to be anxious, which is even more reason to source your puppy from a registered and caring breeder or rescue centre rather than a puppy farm.

Freeze, flight or fight

In a situation where your puppy may feel challenged or insecure, they will instinctively react by freezing, running away or, if they cannot perform either of the first two, exhibiting aggression. The fight response is rarely seen in a young puppy, who will usually respond nervously by staying still in the hope that they will go unnoticed while the frightening stimulus passes. This is a natural behaviour and should be ignored as it is quickly replaced by investigative interest.

Owners who force puppies into frightening or stressful situations may stimulate unwanted reactions, resulting in behavioural problems.

Poor socialization and habituation

If your puppy is not properly exposed to many different people, places, objects and experiences from a very early age, they can develop into a dog with a fear of anything unknown (see pages 84–5).

Unwitting reinforcement

Your puppy will exhibit some degree of fear or nervousness during their normal development into adulthood. It is regularly reported that owners of adolescent dogs (6–14 months) can go through a second fearful stage and need support in getting past it. The difference between a puppy that develops into a confident mature dog and one that lives in a perpetual state of anxiety can sometimes be down to the response of their owner. Giving a nervous puppy a little reassurance with comforting words to support them overcoming a rational or irrational fear is one thing, but coddling them by scooping them up in those moments can instead stop them from ever overcoming fears naturally and lead to a nervous and anxious adult dog. As long as they are safe, there is no danger in staying neutral and calm, allowing time for your puppy to understand and adjust to something fearful with a few words of reassurance.

Poor judgement

Reprimanding your puppy when they cower away from something or someone or exposing them to unruly dogs or frightening environments can lead to them developing an increasingly nervous disposition. Always keep in mind that your puppy is young and naive, and that you are completely in control of to whom and what they are exposed. One bad decision resulting in a frightening experience cause your impressionable young puppy to be scared for life.

Prevention

Socialization and habituation

From as early as eight weeks of age, expose your puppy to as many different types of people and household items as possible. Puppies are very impressionable creatures in the early stages of life, and this trait should be taken advantage of. By bribing them with attention and treats to give them a rush of endorphins (happy hormones) and making any novel situation positive, you can nurture the development of your puppy into a calm and confident dog.

Help overcome fear

Train yourself to neither coddle nor condemn your puppy for nervous behaviour, but to instead give them the chance to overcome fears on their own. Always assess a situation wisely before rushing in to comfort or reprimand your puppy. If they aren't in actual physical danger, then give them time to conquer their fears, which will be quickly replaced with a puppy's normal investigative interest.

Be Calm

Be a patient and confident pet parent even as you fight your urge to protect your fur baby, remaining calm and impassive in the face of any potentially frightening situation in order to accurately and rationally assess it. Your puppy will look to you for guidance, so if there is no potential for physical harm, you remaining passive will show them that you are unaffected and they will follow your lead and calm down.

Cure

Desensitization

A wealth of patience is needed to help a nervous puppy overcome their fears and become a more sociable and easy-going dog. Determine what causes your puppy to be nervous, whether it is strangers, other dogs or traffic, and endeavour to desensitize them to these stimuli by retreating to a distance where they are less fearful and more inquisitive, then building up their confidence.

Traffic

A degree of fearful respect for traffic is desirable, although a dog that barks or scurries away at the slightest traffic noise will not be a pleasure to walk in built-up areas, leading to difficulties later in life. Choose a quiet street with a low but steady traffic flow and sit down nearby, allowing your puppy to keep a good distance from the road. Do not reprimand if puppy shows a fearful response; simply talk to them in a soothing, constant tone in your normal speaking voice. Gradually walk them closer to the road's edge over successive weeks, not moving nearer until your puppy is calmly ignoring the passing traffic. Be prepared for this process to take some time and allocate periods to work with your puppy when you also will be feeling calm.

High-value treats

When showing fear, your puppy can be encouraged to feel positively when offered a food they love. Keep their most favourite treats for these moments, to help build positive associations at a distance from the stimulus at which your puppy feels safe.

Strangers

If your puppy is nervous when strangers approach, begin by sitting in a living room, garden or local park where there are people walking by or congregating at a safe distance. Once puppy seems perfectly calm, allow strangers to greet them from a distance without talking to or looking at them. Ask them to advance slowly, then stop a short distance away while throwing a treat in your puppy's direction, giving the puppy time and space to assess the situation and decide whether to meet the person halfway or not. Talk to the strangers during this time in a calm manner, giving them advice on helping your puppy to overcome their nerves, but without giving your puppy undue attention. If your dog is showing overt signs of nervousness, don't allow strangers to treat your dog by hand, as this will simply teach your puppy to push through nervousness to approach strangers even when they're not comfortable to do so. This can lead to nervous aggression or snatching of food.

Other dogs

Puppy-socialization classes should be heavily relied upon to help you and your puppy learn to socialize with other dogs (see page 55). If you are unable to attend one, invite friends and family with dogs that are known to be calm and well-mannered to meet your puppy. Closely monitor the meeting without over-controlling the situation, again taking into account that initial nerves shown by your puppy may be quickly replaced by playful exuberance.

Dogs in the park should always be strictly monitored, as one bad experience could lead to fearful and antisocial tendencies developing in your puppy. Never feel embarrassed to ask other dog owners if their dog is sociable before allowing them to meet your puppy – no meeting at all is better than a frightening one.

Divert attention

Good basic training is a perfect way of taking a dog's mind off a potentially fearful situation. If your puppy appears nervous, command them to 'sit', then offer praise and attention for responding correctly. Initiate a game or give them a treat so that their attention is on you and they are ignoring whatever stimuli may have previously unnerved them.

Medication and alternative therapies

If your puppy suffers with a naturally nervous disposition, there are a number of treatments that may help to soothe them. Oral nutritional supplements containing ashwagandha and relora (a blend of plant extracts from *Magnolia officinalis* and *Phellodendron amurense*) help to relax a pooch without sedating. Other dietary supplements contain amino acids L-theanine and L-tryptophan, and *Piper methysticum*, all of which are known to help support a calm demeanour.

Scent diffusers containing synthetic dog-appeasing pheromone (the scent released from mum's mammary tissue) can work wonders in calming young puppies just settling in to new environments, and have proven results. Invoking that sense of wellbeing experienced when snuggled up to mum, these products can be highly effective in calming a nervous puppy when they first arrive at a new home. Generally available from your vet, dog-appeasing pheromone is a readily available product that can be used to keep your puppy, and even a mature but nervous dog, contented and happy.

Vitamin B deficiency has also been linked to a nervous disposition and can be supplemented either via injection, oral tablets or powders.

For those dogs suffering with serious anxiety issues, veterinarians do prescribe tri-cyclic anti-depressants where necessary, to help reduce nerves and allow a dog to process their emotions and be able to participate in training.

Any medicinal supplements should always be discussed fully with your vet and used in conjunction with behavioural techniques. Best results will be achieved in your puppy when such medicines are used in combination with extra training, improving the bond between you and building up their confidence in all situations.

Travel sickness and car phobia

Confined to a tin box **hurtling from side to side, stopping** without warning, with **images flashing** past and a low **rumbling noise from** below – puppies can understandably find car journeys frightening. Some will be sick on their first few journeys, while others will **whine and shake with fear,** resulting in an **aversion to car travel.**

Why

Motion sickness

Some puppies will suffer from motion sickness, as do some people. This condition is similar to sea sickness and is caused by the sideways movement of fluids within your puppy's inner ear. The movement makes your puppy feel nauseous, sometimes resulting in vomiting. This can be a transient problem or one that haunts your shared car journeys in the long term.

Fear

A puppy can be anxious when exposed to a vehicle for a number of reasons: lack of experience of car travel, a negative association with car trips, such as going to the veterinary clinic, being involved in a car accident or previous experience of travel sickness. Just being confined in a stationary car can evoke a fear response, which can result in excessive vocalization, salivation, panting or vomiting.

Prevention

Early acclimatization

In the first few weeks of ownership, a puppy should not be taken outside the confines of your home and garden unless it is absolutely necessary. However, during this time, it is nevertheless important to acclimatize them to your car. A puppy at this age is in the process of learning about the world around them and is most likely to take the new experience in their stride. If you wait until you are allowed to take puppy for walks, they may be less able to cope with a potentially frightening experience, especially since it is likely that the only car journeys they will have previously experienced will have resulted in them being at the end of a veterinarian's needle!

Brief excursions

From day one, transport your puppy on short journeys in the way that you mean to continue, such as in a pet carry container secured with a seatbelt, in a travel cage in the car's rear compartment or with a harness fitted and attached to a seatbelt in the front or back seat. It should be noted that in the UK and many other countries, it is a legal requirement that a dog be suitably restrained in a car. If you allow puppy to travel on your lap when small, they will understandably be upset when confined and relegated to the rear of the car or back seat when they are older. Keep the car journeys very short and relaxed, offering puppy a treat when the trip is finished to end on a positive note. A daily car journey is ideal, to help foster acceptance of car travel as part of life. Slowly increase the length of the journeys and introduce the occasional interlude out of the car, off the ground and safe from unvaccinated dogs (for example, at a friend's house who doesn't have a dog) at a suitable stopping point en route.

Drive considerately

Moderate your speed when driving, take any bends slowly and smoothly, and avoid shouting or blowing the car horn. This will all help to keep the journey as calm and relaxing as possible for your puppy. Provide fresh air to keep your puppy comfortable, but don't allow them to put their head out of the window as this may result in eye injuries. Avoid smoking, which can lead to nausea in your puppy.

Cure

Slow and steady

Gradually allow your puppy to be exposed to the car and car travel in controlled stages. Firstly, get puppy comfortable with being in the confines of a stationary car. Play games with your puppy in the car to make it a positive and fun place to be. For example, get them to climb in after you in pursuit of a toy or treat, then reward with lots of praise. Once puppy seems happy to be in the car, restrain them in the carry container, cage or harness and offer treats or indeed their whole meal. If you wish, you could even feed all meals in the car for a few days in order to nurture a positive association with being in the car.

Once your puppy accepts being secured in the car, take them on very short trips, just to the end of the road and back, keeping them calm by talking in a constant, reassuring tone. Don't give them any attention in response to nervousness; give praise only when they are sitting quietly without any signs of anxiety.

Make car travel fun

When your puppy is old enough to go for walks, drive them to the park so that they can enjoy a car journey and not have it always ending in a visit to the vet. After a short journey, take your puppy out of the car and play with them; then, on return to your vehicle, offer a treat. These simple actions will reinforce the association of car travel with pleasure. If you have a puppy who is vocal or over-excitable in the car, make sure you exercise them well before returning to your vehicle and avoid giving too much attention when you are driving so that they will settle quietly in the confines of their carry container, cage or harness.

Anti-nausea and anti-anxiety drugs

Used to help manage motion sickness or in cases of severe anxiety as a last resort, there are certain medications that a vet or specialist animal behaviourist may recommend to help an older puppy overcome an irrational car-travel anxiety. All training methods should be completely exhausted before considering this treatment and further habituation is recommended in conjunction with administering them.

Sick as a dog

HEALTHCARE STRATEGIES

Puppies, like young children, can get very sick very quickly. Being able to detect the early warning signs of illness is invaluable for your puppy's wellbeing, as is the ability to deal with minor complaints and emergencies at home. There is no substitute for veterinary treatment, but you may find some of the complementary therapies detailed here worth exploring.

Early warning signs

Your puppy should be a generally **happy and energetic soul, with an eagerness to eat and a willingness to sleep. Being a responsible owner** requires a clear understanding of your puppy's health needs and the ability to **identify accurately the early warning signs** of illness, to ensure a **quick recovery.**

Change in behaviour

The most common cause of owners taking their pets to the vet is a noticeable change in behaviour. Whether they are quieter than usual, having difficulty sleeping or just not their normal playful self, a change in behaviour in your puppy tends to be the most accurate indicator of ill health.

Change in appetite

Try sharpening puppy's appetite

Going off food is a common sign of oncoming illness in a puppy. If they don't seem interested in eating, cover the food and put it away for an hour or two. Returning the food at the next prescribed mealtime will give puppy enough time to have developed an appetite.

Avoid pandering to whims

A fussy puppy will do their utmost to get treats and tasty food all the time and will refuse entire meals in protest at their current diet. Do not automatically supplement their meal with an alternative, as your puppy will forever dictate what you feed them based on whim. They are just like a child who won't eat their greens and you as a puppy parent do know best. If you stick to a good-quality diet and don't weaken, the likelihood is that they will eat it at the next mealtime. If puppy still doesn't eat, consider adding warm water to try to improve its smell and palatability. If the problem continues, considering phoning your vet for guidance.

Change in temperature

A shivering or panting puppy that feels overly warm to the touch will benefit from immediate veterinary advice or attention. Some owners may choose to keep a digital thermometer at home for their own use and for when their puppy's temperature is in question. As the temperature of a sharp-toothed puppy can only safely be taken rectally or aurally (from the ear), you should receive training in the sterile and safe use of a thermometer by veterinary staff before trying this at home.

While a warm nose in a puppy is traditionally seen as a sign of ill health, the reality is that a puppy may have a cold nose yet still be suffering from a fever. The only true measure of a puppy's temperature is a thermometer. The average body temperature of a puppy is 38.1–39.2°C (100.5–102.5°F), with temperatures of 39.5°C (103.1°F) and over described as feverish.

Use the puppy health check (see page 28) to familiarize yourself with the characteristics of a healthy puppy. Being able to quickly assess your puppy's general health at home means that, when necessary, you can provide pertinent information to your vet to help them deliver accurate treatment for a swift recovery.

Common puppy illnesses

Many relatively **minor health problems** can be **prevented from** developing if **warning signs** are picked up **early** and swiftly, using **simple treatment at home. Some will require investigation and treatment** at a **veterinary clinic, but** your daily vigilance will again **pay dividends** in your puppy receiving **prompt attention.**

Anaemia

Diagnosed chiefly by pale-pink or white gums, rapid breathing and weakness, anaemia is a lower than normal level of red blood cells in your puppy's vascular system. Mostly the result of high worm or flea burdens in a young puppy, anaemia can also be caused by bleeding wounds, poisons, toxins and immune reactions. If you suspect anaemia, the condition must be assessed immediately by your vet and treatment will almost certainly be needed to return your puppy to good health.

Constipation

A puppy should normally pass a few bowel motions every day. Constipation is diagnosed when your puppy does not pass faecal material for an extended period, resulting in accumulation in the lower bowels, a bloated abdomen and discomfort. This condition commonly occurs after a change in diet to a higher-fibre alternative and can be relieved by mineral oil supplements, such as paraffin/malt products or faecal-softening, bulk-forming agents at home, or a small enema preparation at your vet clinic. Prevention can be as simple as stimulating your puppy to drink more by softening any dry food with warm water.

Coughing

Apart from a brief fit suffered after the speedy consumption of food or water, a coughing puppy should always be taken to a vet for examination. Varying greatly in cause, coughs can be dry or wet in nature, productive or non-productive, or associated with ocular (eye), oral (mouth) or nasal discharges. Coughing can be caused by infections, foreign bodies or injury to or abnormal function of the lungs or heart, and accurate diagnosis is required to treat it effectively.

Kennel cough

This is one disease commonly known to cause coughing in young puppies. Contracted from breeding establishments, dog walking groups, parks or other high-concentration dog areas, kennel cough is caused by a handful of viral diseases that are highly contagious. It causes a dry, 'smokers'-type cough, and can be further complicated by infection of the bacterium *Bordetella bronchiseptica*, resulting in a purulent nasal discharge and a reduced appetite.

Kennel cough can be prevented by vaccination, and treated with anything from symptomatic preparations (cough syrup) and anti-inflammatories to specific antibiotic medications. The condition usually resolves around ten days after infection, although symptoms will be improved during that time by medication.

Diarrhoea

Soft bowel motions are a common condition in puppies and should be monitored closely. A puppy suffering with diarrhoea lasting longer than one or two stools should be referred to your vet immediately for treatment, since the condition can result in sudden dehydration. Diarrhoea is commonly caused by a change in diet or consuming rich or unsanitary food. A bright and otherwise healthy puppy can be monitored at home with food restriction for a few hours and plenty of fresh water available.

If diarrhoea continues, or your puppy seems lethargic or blood is present in the faeces, a consultation with your vet is advisable to treat the problem swiftly. A parasitic or bacterial infection can cause severe diarrhoea, which can require your puppy to be hospitalized to correct dehydration or anaemia while the cause is treated specifically.

Ear problems

Examining your puppy daily is key to preventing problems affecting the ears. Commonly occurring in floppy- or large-eared dogs such as bassets or cocker spaniels, ear problems tend to be caused by infection, parasites or foreign bodies. Regular cleaning with cotton wool and ear-cleaning preparations is highly effective in minimizing wax levels, which once accumulated can lead to infection or parasite infestation. Checking inside your puppy's ears daily after walks can prevent the need for painful removal of foreign bodies from the ear canal by your vet at a later stage. If puppy's ears have a strong smell, or there is lots of dark or yellow build-up in the ear canals, a vet visit is needed to provide effective treatment for potential fungal, bacterial or parasitic infections.

Eye problems

Eye problems are common to flat-faced (brachycephalic) breeds such as French bulldogs and pugs, and injury and infection are the most likely causes in a growing puppy. Keeping a regular check on your puppy's eyes is paramount to ensuring healthy vision as they grow.

Conjunctivitis is the most common cause of ocular discharge in puppies, and infection or injury requires a prompt visit to your vet. Dark discharge from the eyes on a daily basis is normal, like 'sleep' that accumulates in our eyes when waking in the morning. Puppies naturally have brown/red coloured tears, and this build-up can be cleaned away from their eyes with moist cotton wool. Yellow or green discharge signifies infection and should be assessed by your vet.

Hair loss

Patches of hair loss (alopecia) that appear on your puppy should be closely monitored. Mites, fleas, allergy and bacterial or fungal infections can all cause a puppy to be intensely itchy or result in alopecia, developing most commonly over the ears, flanks, abdomen and tail. If not treated quickly, hair loss can worsen dramatically in a scratching puppy, with secondary infections being introduced to the damaged skin.

Preventative treatment

Home treatment with anti-parasitic medications prescribed by your vet should prevent the majority of skin irritations (see page 62), although if your puppy seems overly itchy or hair loss develops, make an appointment to see your vet, as allergies to food or environment may be materializing.

Mouth and teeth problems

Many owners will be disturbed by a puppy's loss of baby (deciduous) teeth, which can occur from around three months of age. Bleeding gums can also result when puppy chews on their toys. However, both these symptoms are normal as the puppy's adult teeth grow through.

Checking your puppy's mouth regularly and training them to be comfortable with this examination is essential in keeping their oral cavity in pristine condition. Learning how to brush your puppy's teeth daily is an excellent way to ensure healthy teeth and gums throughout their life.

This also allows you to check your puppy's mouth in general, and to detect any problems that your vet should assess.

Warning signs

Signs that your puppy is unable to eat or is shying away from food require prompt investigation; fractured teeth due to chewing hard surfaces, foreign bodies, gum injury, bad breath or infection are all conditions that need veterinary attention.

Urinary disorders

Occurring infrequently in puppies, urine infections can be detected by owners through a change in the colour or consistency of the urine. A puppy that passes urine more or less frequently than normal could be suffering from a urinary infection, irritation or abnormality, so seek advice from your vet. Familiarizing yourself with the colour and consistency of your puppy's urine may be a little unpleasant, but has been proven an accurate tool in diagnosing urinary problems quickly at home.

The most common cause of a urinary disorder is bacterial cystitis, which will cause your puppy to strain and produce cloudy urine. This should be treated specifically according to the diagnosis made by your vet based on the urine (so catch a sample if you are able) and will quickly resolve once your puppy is prescribed the correct course of antibiotics.

Vomiting

The forceful projection of digested food or gut contents from the mouth is known as vomiting. Many owners confuse vomiting with the act of bringing up undigested food, which is known as regurgitation and is commonly observed in puppies. Regurgitation tends to be a physical response to over-eating, grass consumption or poor settling of food contents in the stomach. It differs from vomiting in that your puppy will suddenly bring up his stomach contents, then feel bright and happy, recommencing eating with no lingering side effects.

Vomiting tends to be physiological in nature as a result of nausea and is an attempt by the body to rid itself of the cause. Your puppy will tend to be a little depressed after vomiting and will abstain from eating for a short period. Caused by the consumption of foreign bodies, rotting food or poisonous materials, metabolic disease, infection or other nausea-causing conditions, vomiting should always be discussed with your vet as it can quickly lead to dehydration.

Nursing your sick puppy

Once your vet has examined your sick puppy, only in the most severe cases will it be necessary for them to be kept at the vet clinic. After being sent home with medication and advice, your unwell puppy will need lots of tender loving care and patience to help them to recover as quickly as possible.

What you can do

Provide warmth and quiet

Place your unwell puppy in a warmer part of the house, away from doors and draughts. Your puppy will recover better in a quiet environment, so place them in their puppy crate or playpen lined with blankets and possibly a heat mat or hot-water bottle. Keep noise to a minimum and boisterous children and other pets away to give your puppy the chance to rest and recuperate.

Provide the right food and water

If your puppy is suffering from a poor appetite, your vet may suggest alternative foods to stimulate them to eat. Be careful not to change your puppy's diet too dramatically, as this may lead to diarrhoea and further complicate matters. Warming up food using hot water, thereby improving its smell, can be an effective way of stimulating appetite. Clean drinking water must be available at all times.

Administer medication with care

Listen to your vet's advice and always read the labels before giving medication to your sick puppy. Measure out the dosage of tablets or liquid oral medication before administering and place it down the throat or mix it with food according to your vet's recommendation. If you aren't sure, it is always worth double checking to make sure you have it right.

Creams, drops or ointments should be applied with the help of a family member or friend, and the area of treatment cleaned well before and after to avoid a build-up of debris.

For safety reasons, make sure you keep all puppy medication out of the reach of children and any animals in the house.

Give toilet help

As your puppy may be too weak to go to the toilet normally, house-training may have to take a backward step. At regular intervals pick up your puppy and take them to where you would like them to go. Afford your puppy extra patience and time in toileting while they are unwell.

Monitor their condition

Keep a very close eye on your puppy's progress, monitoring eating, drinking and toileting habits to ensure that puppy is getting better. Keep your vet clinic's phone numbers to hand and call for advice if your puppy is not improving or their condition seems to be deteriorating.

Puppy first aid

The home can be a treacherous place for your unsuspecting yet inquisitive and adventurous young puppy, with many dangers lurking indoors and out to catch them unawares. Accidents and injuries need to be dealt with quickly and effectively by you, ensuring immediate safety and preventing further injury until puppy arrives at the veterinary clinic.

In an emergency

Stay calm

First aid for your puppy can potentially save their life and is something that every responsible owner should learn. The number-one rule is don't panic! Take a moment to collect yourself, act calmly and think things through rationally. Never give your puppy human medications, which may complicate matters. Also avoid offering any food, because an empty stomach is advisable for a general anaesthetic, which may be needed on arrival at the veterinary clinic for certain procedures.

Safety first

Think before you act, as your safety is as important as that of your puppy. If you act rashly and injure yourself, you could place your puppy further in peril as you may be the only person in the vicinity able to help them. Injured puppies that are frightened and in pain may try to bite anyone who touches them, including their owner.

First, assess the situation, then remove pup from immediate danger (for example, off the road) using a thick towel or blanket, which you should keep in the boot of your vehicle in case of emergencies. Failing that, you could use a jacket or coat if you are wearing one. Contact your vet immediately. Keep your vet's phone number to hand, ideally programmed into your mobile phone, but make sure you know the name of the vet's practice in case you need to find the number. Always phone ahead, as vets are not fully resident at their clinics and may need to travel to help you or recommend an out-of-hours hospital for you to attend instead. Staff at the clinic will be able to give you advice as to what immediate action you should take.

Basic examination

A quick examination of your puppy is extremely useful when describing to the vet clinic the injuries that they may have sustained. Again with your own safety in mind, attempt to check the gums (they should be pink) and breathing (normal, laboured or noisy); then assess for pain, ability to walk (lameness) and any discharges present. This information can quickly pinpoint your puppy's injury or illness and allow your vet to provide you with appropriate first-aid measures.

External bleeding

Caused by any number of injuries such as grazes, wounds or cuts, external bleeding is something that needs to be dealt with quickly. Apply pressure over the site with your hand or a bandage from your puppy first-aid kit (see pages 234–5). If blood seeps through the first bandage, apply another one on top, as replacing the first bandage will remove the clot that has formed and bleeding will recommence. Don't apply a tourniquet unless bleeding seems to be unrelenting, as there is a danger of stopping circulation to the affected area, which may potentially result in loss of the limb. Do your best to keep your puppy as quiet and still as possible while you call your vet.

Once the bleeding has stopped, clean the wound with warm, salty water. Don't use any household cleaners or human products.

Internal bleeding

This can occur as a result of a road-traffic accident (RTA) and symptoms can include: bleeding from the nose, mouth or rectum; coughing blood; blood in the urine; pale gums; collapse; rapid or weak pulse. If you suspect internal bleeding, keep your puppy as warm and quiet as possible during transit to your veterinary clinic.

Bite wounds

Sustained by only the most unlucky of puppies, bite wounds are not only painful but can quickly become infected unless the treatment is swift. After you have applied pressure to control any bleeding, you should assess the wound by clearing fur away from the site using clippers or scissors. If the skin has not been punctured, the use of antiseptic cleaners may be all the treatment that is necessary. A full-thickness puncture wound of the skin will need more intensive treatment, with proper irrigation and a course of antibiotics prescribed by your vet to avoid infection.

Burns and scalds

Puppies do have a tendency to run under feet and scalds from hot drinks are periodically seen in the vet clinic. Burns caused by spitting oil, indoor fireplaces or from jumping up onto hot surfaces can also occur. If this unfortunate fate befalls your puppy, take first-aid measures similar to those that you would use in the case of humans, such as applying a cold compress or immersion in water.

In the freakish event that your puppy is actually on fire, then the first action you take should obviously be to smother the flames immediately using a fire blanket, coat, rug or other suitable item. If you can, clean off whatever has caused the burn, such as oil or barbecue embers, then immerse the burned area in cold water for approximately ten minutes. Remove anything that could constrict the site, such as a collar. However, you should leave the collar in place if it has been burned (unless it is causing breathing difficulties) to avoid causing any further damage to the puppy's burned skin.

After you have bathed the burns, keep your puppy warm as burns can then counter-intuitively lead to hypothermia, and cover the affected area with a saline-moistened dressing. You should avoid applying any topical creams or pain-relief medication until you are able to seek veterinary advice and treatment.

Breathing difficulties

Many situations may cause a puppy to have difficulty breathing and restrict their oxygen supply. Check gum colour – a bluish hue indicates a severe respiratory emergency.

Drowning

This can occur when puppies are left unattended around water, such as pools, ponds and baths. If your puppy has swallowed a lot of water, first hold them upside down until all the water drains away. Only then can their lungs fill with life-giving air.

Choking

If you can see an object in the mouth, hold your puppy firmly in a towel and use a pair of forceps or something similar to remove it gently. Never pull something if it is lodged, especially swallowed string, which may concertina the intestines causing massive internal damage. If possible, take your puppy immediately to the vet.

Electric shock

Electrocution is the likely result of chewing power cables. Don't touch your puppy until the electricity has been turned off, using a dry, non-metallic item such as a broom handle to push them away from the power source. Consider giving artificial respiration if breathing has stopped and call your vet.

Fits

If this uncommon event occurs, ensure your safety and the safety of your puppy by not trying to soothe or intervene until your puppy recovers. Move all furniture and electrical appliances out of the way, turn off any music and draw the blinds or curtains to create a calm, subdued environment. Some seizures will last for just a few seconds, but some can continue for minutes. Afterwards, your puppy will slowly regain consciousness, although they will remain recumbent and weak. Extend the neck to facilitate an open airway, loosen any collar worn and call the vet immediately.

RESUSCITATION

Expired air resuscitation (EAR) and cardiopulmonary resuscitation (CPR) are best left to the professionals, but if your puppy has stopped breathing and no help is available, then you may need to come to their aid.

1 Lay the puppy on their right side with neck extended and head slightly lower than the rest of the body. Check the airway for obstructions, clearing out any saliva or debris from the mouth with your hand (if your puppy is a victim of drowning, you should remove the water from the lungs by holding them upside down). Assess if the puppy is breathing by watching their abdomen, which should rise and fall, or place a piece of hair or grass in front of their nose to see if it moves. If there is no sign of breathing, you may need to resuscitate your puppy by using artificial respiration.

2 Close your puppy's mouth by holding their nose with one hand while extending the neck. Make a tube with your other hand and exhale a puff of air through the nose to expand puppy's chest at a frequency of 15–20 times per minute (once every 3–4 seconds).

3 Remove your mouth after each breath and check for signs of breathing. It is also important to check for a heartbeat, either by gently squeezing over the heart to feel its beat directly or by checking for the femoral pulse. The heart can be located at around the point of the elbow in relation to the chest on the left-hand side. The femoral artery is a large artery found on the inside surface of the back legs/thighs and is easily palpated in dogs for the assessment of pulse.

4 If you are certain there is no pulse, commence CPR. Firmly squeeze the chest at the point of the elbow, making 15 compressions per 10 seconds (for an average-sized dog) to stimulate the heart to begin pumping again. Two breaths exhaled through the nose, as in Step 2, should follow in quick succession. Repeat the cycle for one minute. Check again for breathing and pulse every minute. Once the puppy is breathing on their own, dry them off if wet and keep them warm. Seek professional assistance as soon as possible.

Warning You should use EAR and CPR only as a last resort, if professional help is not available, as the techniques can lead to injury of your puppy or yourself. These hints are not a substitute for professional assistance or proper study of first aid.

Insect stings and bites

An inquisitive puppy can easily suffer a painful bite or sting in the garden or park. If a sting can be seen, remove it below the bulbous poison sac using tweezers, then bathe the area with cool water or apply ice to soothe the pain. A solution of bicarbonate of soda for bee stings and vinegar for wasp stings are traditional remedies that are effective in neutralizing the poison. If a sting is present around the throat or mouth, visit your vet immediately as swelling may interfere with your puppy's ability to breathe.

Snake or spider bites

If your puppy has been bitten by a venomous snake or spider, try to identify the culprit as best you can. Raise the affected limb or body part, pick your puppy up and quickly transport them to the vet for immediate treatment.

Lameness

When a puppy is seen limping you should immediately assess the affected limb. Gently check the whole leg from top to bottom for injuries, foreign bodies or deformities that may require veterinary attention. The worst example of lameness is due to broken bones. Falls or injuries indoors can lead to fractures, although the most common cause of broken bones in dogs is road traffic accidents.

A broken bone can be detected by pain, swelling at the site, unnatural movement of the puppy's leg, deformity or a grating noise when touched. The most prudent first aid is minimal – touch the fracture site only if you are attempting to stem any bleeding. Pick your puppy up using a thick towel or blanket, with the injured leg uppermost, and then place them in a padded carry container or box for transportation to your vet. Do not supply pain relief at home, but call your vet for advice before driving safely to the veterinary clinic.

Remember that your puppy will bite to defend themselves, and will bite if you touch a sore area of their body. If you have access to a muzzle, place it on your puppy before examining them to ensure that you don't get injured in the process.

Temperature extremes

Your puppy can be very sensitive to changes in temperature and even limited exposure to extremes of hot and cold temperatures may cause them distress.

Hyperthermia

Commonly known as heat stroke, this potentially lethal condition is mainly seen when puppies are left in hot cars or unventilated rooms. Usually quite obvious, symptoms of a puppy suffering from heat stroke include panting, excessive salivation and distress. The best treatment is immediate immersion in cool water or draping a wet towel around your puppy to lower their temperature. Don't fully immerse your puppy in water as it can cause shock and lead to drowning; instead, stand them in knee-deep water and cup it over their body to bring their temperature down safely.

Offer puppy cold water to drink once recovered and monitor them closely while gaining further advice from your veterinary clinic. It is always worth visiting your vet if you are concerned that your puppy may have suffered with heat stroke, as depression of the bone marrow and resulting anaemia in the days after the event are commonly reported.

Hypothermia

This is generally caused when a puppy is immersed in cold water, exposed to the elements for excessive periods of time, or accidentally confined outdoors in winter and unable to re-enter your home. A shivering puppy should be quickly dried off with towels and then warmed up slowly with multiple layers of blankets wrapped around them. Avoid attempting to warm your puppy up too quickly using hot-water bottles, as they may burn if applied directly to cold skin.

Poisoning

There are a surprising number of substances lurking in the home that are toxic to your puppy. The best treatment for poisoning is prevention – keep human medications in an inaccessible cupboard or cabinet, chocolate in the refrigerator or an out-of-reach cupboard, and avoid cultivating poisonous plants or trees in the home and garden (see page 234). The common signs of poisoning can include vomiting, diarrhoea, nausea, drooling, seizures and dullness. Don't try to make your puppy sick, but allow them to drink plenty of water as they may try to make themselves vomit.

Common causes of poisoning include:

Coat contamination

Poisoning can result if your puppy contaminates their coat by rubbing on a toxic substance, then begins to clean off the residue by licking. Oil, grease or anti-freeze can be consumed in this way and are extremely dangerous. If such a substance has found its way onto your puppy's coat or paws, do not allow them to lick the area.

Wash the coat with soapy water or clip off the hair if the substance can't be removed. Never use turpentine or paint removers; washing-up liquid is a suitable product to apply. Always discuss potential toxic ingestion with your vet, watching your puppy closely to avoid further consumption of the contaminants during the journey to the vet.

Chocolate

A common cause of poisoning in puppies around Christmas or Easter is eating chocolate. Chocolate is also present in many other food products, such as cakes and biscuits, and must always be kept out of reach of a hungry pup. Cocoa contains an ingredient called theobromine that makes chocolate toxic to dogs, causing vomiting, internal bleeding, seizures and even death. The darker the chocolate, the more theobromine it may contain and the smaller the quantity that needs to be consumed for there to be cause for concern. Always discuss chocolate consumption with your vet, trying to locate any packaging and determine how much they have eaten, helping to guide your vet as to whether medical treatment is necessary.

Plants and trees

Some plants and trees are poisonous to dogs. Ask advice from your vet or garden centre to ensure that your home and garden are free from poisonous varieties. If you are a keen gardener and want to keep these plants in place, erect suitable fencing to keep puppy at bay. Plants that are poisonous to dogs include:

aloe vera
avocado
cyclamen
ferns
hydrangea
ivy
lilies
poinsettia
yucca

Puppy first-aid kit

A first-aid kit is a necessity when owning a dog. It is best kept in a hard plastic container inside a convenient waist bag or backpack, as many injuries are sustained when your puppy is out on walks. The contents should include:

- white open-weave bandages of varying sizes
- adhesive bandages
- cotton wool

- swabs
- lint and gauze
- melanin (non-stick) wound dressings of varying sizes
- clean pieces of cotton sheeting
- small wash bottle containing saline solution
- tweezers
- round-ended scissors
- thermometer
- antiseptic cream or liquid
- mobile phone

Puppy emergency plan

Do

- Keep calm and use common sense
- Puppy-proof your home and garden (see pages 44–9)
- Study first aid further
- Have a first-aid kit to hand and keep it well stocked
- Keep your vet's emergency phone numbers accessible, for example programmed into your mobile phone

Don't

- Panic
- Allow your puppy access to medicines, poisonous substances or rubbish
- Allow your puppy to chew small toys or anything else that could be swallowed
- Ignore warning signs – contact your vet for advice if you are at all

concerned about your puppy's wellbeing

- Be complacent – puppies can quickly get themselves into trouble by meeting aggressive dogs in the park, falling into water, straying onto roads or wandering outside in the cold

Canine therapies

There are a number of medications and therapies that are not provided in smaller, local veterinary practices but that can help to improve your dog's health and wellbeing. Many treatments known to be beneficial in human medicine can have the same positive effects in our fur babies, so be mindful that there is a world of therapy out there to help your new bestie live their best possible life.

Acupuncture

How it works

One of the most widely accepted forms of alternative treatment in Western medicine, acupuncture is a 2,000-year-old technique originally developed by the Chinese. Fine sterilized needles are inserted at specific points along the body's life-energy streams (*chi*), in order to correct their flow when disrupted by injury or disease. Acupuncture's primary action is via the central nervous system, and it is used to treat a variety of disorders – musculoskeletal, dermatological, reproductive, hormonal, gastrointestinal, respiratory and cardiovascular. Its main use in human and animal medicine is for relief of pain, such as that suffered during joint, bone, muscle or ligament injury.

Treatment

After initial sensitivity to the needles, acupuncture causes the release of endorphins, which are the body's natural painkillers, leading to a relaxed puppy who will occasionally fall asleep mid-treatment. Canine patients are treated in a home or clinical environment in approximately 40-minute sessions once or twice weekly for about six weeks. Specialist veterinary acupuncturists practise via vet referral, working to treat pain and other illnesses as an adjunct to conventional treatment.

Aromatherapy

How it works

Experts in alternative medicine for animals believe that some essential oils, extracted from flowers, leaves, stems, roots, seeds and bark, not only improve wellbeing through the sense of smell but also have therapeutic uses in treating a number of canine conditions. Essential oils have been used to treat a long list of illnesses and infections in dogs, from flatulence to motion sickness, bad breath (halitosis) and itchy skin.

Treatment

Aromatherapy should only be used after consultation with your vet regarding the specific condition. Essential oils must always be diluted with an oil base (such as olive oil) or a mixture of distilled water, glycerine and vodka, and never applied in pure form. As these medications are highly concentrated and your puppy has an acute sense of smell, they must be used sparingly, at around 25 per cent of an adult human dose. If you are interested in using aromatherapy to treat your puppy, ask your vet about contacting a respected alternative-therapies practitioner in your area before beginning any home treatment. These treatments can be used in conjunction with traditional medicine and should not be substituted for it without consultation with your veterinary surgeon.

Hydrotherapy

How it works

Hydrotherapy is a non-weight-bearing form of exercise designed to rehabilitate dogs – basically swimming for pooches. The treatment is rapidly growing in popularity and gaining widespread support from the veterinary community. Hydrotherapy is ideal for dogs that are suffering from degenerative joint diseases such as arthritis or hip dysplasia and it is also very effective in fighting canine obesity and supporting recovery from orthopaedic procedures.

Treatment

Participants are placed in buoyant harnesses and then walked into a pool by trained staff. High-powered underwater jets are used to create currents and a low-impact workout. In some cases, owners are able to share the experience and benefits with their pet. Sessions last for about 20 minutes and are relatively inexpensive – in some cases, the cost is covered by pet insurance. Ask your local veterinary surgery for advice on the closest facility.

Massage and physiotherapy

How it works

Specialist veterinary physiotherapists are working closely with a number of veterinary practices to speed recovery in dogs following accident and injury. Practitioners also teach owners massage techniques that they can use at home to help their dogs recover from training and exercise or to assist relaxation. These techniques are becoming more widespread, although permission from your vet should always be sought before consultation.

Treatment

Physiotherapists provide appropriate manipulation and massage techniques to help reduce pain, stimulate circulation and lymphatic drainage, relax muscles, and increase joint mobility and range of motion in their canine patients. Pet insurance will often cover veterinary physiotherapy fees, as these techniques are proven to improve the recovery times of dogs suffering from injuries and requiring rehabilitation.

WOOF!

Five things that dogs do that most pet parents misinterpret

Here I lift the lid on some very common pet-parent fails when it comes to reading canine body language. Communication with a person that cannot speak our language can prove very challenging, but with the use of lots of subtle and not so subtle hand signals and body language, we can hope to get the gist of what they are trying to tell us. The same applies to our dogs, who use a complex array of body positions to try to get their pooch point across. If your dog is feeling happy or anxious, excited or content, they will use a variety of conscious and unconscious signals to communicate with us.

It is then down to us to interpret them…That's where the problems start!

So often dogs perform actions or gestures that we either misinterpret or miss entirely – and trust me when I say that after 25 years of being a vet there are still times when even I get it wrong. So rather than trying to understand all the complex language of body signals that our emotive canines may, well, *emote*, instead let's start with a list of the five behaviours most commonly misread by dog owners.

1 Tail wagging

Now this surely means a happy dog that is friendly and wants to say hi? Not necessarily. Frequently misinterpreted as a sign of happiness, the wag of a canine's tail can be as a result of feeling aroused, over-stimulated or frustrated. Focusing just on the tail is like listening to only part of a sentence, making it pretty hard to interpret what someone is telling you. So the entire body language of your pup must be taken into account. When they are confident or aroused, the tail is held high to expose their scent glands, which are either side of the anus, to advertise their presence with good airflow around the area. If the tail is wagging side to side but pooch seems tense with hard, staring eyes, then this could indicate an overly aroused or frustrated dog that is best left alone. A slower-wagged tail can indicate a canine that is calmly assessing a situation and should be given time and space to do so. A helicopter-style 360-degree wag is a sure-fire sign of friendliness, with a relaxed stance and bum wiggling likely to suggest that this is a dog who definitely wants to say hi.

2 Yawning

Yawning is a clear sign of tiredness or relaxation in us humans but rather the opposite in dogs, where it is most commonly an indicator of stress. Of course dogs do yawn when they are tired, but they are more likely to yawn when they are nervous or experiencing fear. Take a moment to assess the situation and try to appease your dog's stress or discomfort, offering a calm approach to help reduce your canine companion's jangling nerves.

3 Lip licking or smacking

In humans, this is normally a signal that a great meal is about to be had or has just been consumed; a sign of comfort or contentment. In dogs, it is invariably the polar opposite, commonly a sign of nausea or an appeasement gesture when our dogs perceive a threat and wish to avoid injury. A canine that may have consumed something highly fatty or degenerate may start lip smacking before vomiting, with some metabolic conditions such as pancreatitis or liver disease having a similar effect. In cases of social nervousness or fear, lip smacking is a non-threatening behaviour designed to de-escalate and diffuse a situation to avoid injury, and is key for survival in wild dog packs.

4 Teeth chattering

Inappropriate clothing on a winter's day or a dip in some cold water could lead to chattering of teeth in us humans and is a clear sign of feeling cold. In your pooch it is likely to suggest that they are either suffering with dental disease or are feeling a little nervous. This displacement gesture helps a nervous dog refocus their attention away from a perceived or actual threat and in essence is a self-calming behaviour. Along with sneezing, shaking, sniffing or excessive nose licking, teeth chattering can become a compulsive behaviour that should not be ignored and may need the help of specialist animal behaviourists to understand and effectively address the issue.

5 Exposed tummy

It is hard to resist an exposed fluffy pooch tummy if you are a dog lover, but the exposed tummy itself is not always an invitation to touch. In some cases, this is behaviour performed by a nervous dog to show deference as they try to retreat from the interaction, and a tummy rub can result in an aggressive response. Often this behaviour, when associated with a relaxed body and slightly open mouth with tongue lolling out, is exactly what you would expect: a trusting signal inviting a tummy rub and some social contact.

BEWARE

Ten things humans do that dogs don't understand

Puppy parenting can be tricky to get right – and while our dogs are part of the family, they are not human and therefore do need to be treated differently.

Whether Fido is flummoxed by your attempts at affection, your canine confused by your need for eye contact or your doggo is distraught by your extended departure, perturbed pooches everywhere can find us humans hard to fathom. In an attempt to help guide you through the sometimes intimidating but always interesting world of canine behaviour, here is a list of the many things that humans do – intentionally or totally unconsciously – that our furry four-legged friends find confusing.

10 Coddling

Coddling, or offering excessive emotional and physical comfort when your dog is nervous or stressed, can sometimes lead to a higher risk of anxiety and behavioural issues. A certain amount of structure and discipline is a good thing, but excessive love and affection without order can be confusing and actually worsen anxiety. Anxious behaviours are ignored by wild dog pack leaders, who give off a sense of calm confidence and expect it to be followed; hence if a dog is given excessive attention in a domestic environment when they are nervous, it can reinforce that type of behaviour rather than reduce and resolve it. Barking, noise phobias, separation anxiety and over-protective behaviours need to be dealt with carefully. Offering reassurance without excessive affection when your dog is nervous is completely fair enough; rewarding positive behaviours such as being quiet and calm is the right way to go and avoids accidentally reinforcing the negative, which can lead to insecurity, fear and, in some cases, aggression.

9 Staring

'Don't stare, it's rude', your mother used to say – and dogs would agree with her. Locking eyes with a pooch for a prolonged period can be taken as a challenge, making them feel confused and uncomfortable, causing anxiety or even leading to an aggressive snap. You have been warned.

8 Patting on the head

Dog lovers love dogs, right? But we need to learn how to greet dogs properly. Standing over them and patting them on the head without warning can be frightening and should be avoided. It is far better to introduce yourself to their human instead, asking for permission to approach their canine companion before bounding in. Crouching down with your hands to yourself and allowing a strange dog to come to you is the best way to avoid stressing them out – and losing a finger. Give guidance to others when approaching your puppy to ensure that the interaction is a positive one, as the person would have intended.

7 Hugging

A good bear hug may be good for, well, a *bear*...but dogs don't generally show affection that way. A firm embrace can be perceived by a canine as them being restrained and can feel awkward or dominating to them. Your dog may love your hugs, but this will not be their preferred expression of affection from strangers.

6 Yelling

No one and nothing likes being yelled at: a sharp, shrill or booming increase in vocal volume is associated with anger in many species. Rather than simply raising your voice, consider the use of tone changes to get your point across. A deep tone helps to instruct and gain attention, while higher-pitched tones can be a sign that fun, games and treats may be on offer.

5 Teasing

Dogs may be funny and make us laugh constantly, but they haven't got the best sense of humour. Teasing with a toy or pretending to throw a ball and then not doing so can be baffling to downright annoying and encourage insecurity, irritation and even aggression. Some playful games such as tug-of-war can be OK as long as you win more than you lose. A key message when training children to live alongside canines should definitely be: 'Don't tease the dog.'

4 Punishing past behaviours

Finding a 'present' on the carpet or a favourite pair of shoes chewed on your return home can test the very best of us, but telling your dog off about it after the fact is pointless. Canines are unable to reflect on what they have done and will just believe you are unhappy with them in that very moment, leading to feelings of confusion and fear, and ultimately driving a wedge in the relationship between you and your beloved fur baby. Training is all about patience and knowledge, and punishing past behaviours is an area our canine friends are crucially not equipped to process. Instead you will need to learn to let bygones be bygones when it comes to your furry bestie's past indiscretions. Consider a stress ball or punch bag if you need to expel your annoyance without losing your temper with them.

3 Me time

Your canine is a social creature, enjoying the feeling of being part of a pack in the wild, and thrives on social contact. 'Me time' is a common phrase to suggest enjoying one's own company but this is not a concept to which your canine companion can relate. Long periods left home alone can lead to behavioural issues such as soiling, vocalizing or self-trauma; and even short times left alone can be a source of anxiety for many dogs. If you ensure that you and your dog spend some time apart when you are in the house together, you can reasonably expect them to be comfortable home alone for at least a short amount of time. Consider dog walkers and doggy day care for long days spent away from your pooch, with an exciting array of interactive toys and treats to keep your dog stimulated mentally and physically when you need to head out more briefly.

2 Inconsistency

Dogs like to know where they stand, and having clear rules to abide by is key to having a calm and contented canine. Within a household, rules on your pooch's behaviour must be clear and upheld by all humans at all times. Allowing your dog to be on the bed one day and not the next is confusing and can lead to anxiety for both you and them.

And the number one thing that we do that dogs don't understand is...

1 Changing routines

Dogs are creatures of habit and they enjoying know what's what and when. Any variation in their feeding, walking or playtime schedules can lead to anxiety and stress, so do them a favour and keep to the same routine as much as possible. Your pup will appreciate it.

BETTY AND SKULLY'S DIARY
Living happily ever after

The first six months that I spent with these two pups were a true test of patience and a journey of enlightenment. Betty grew into a happy and well-adjusted dog who loved people and other dogs, and was incredibly loyal, adorably sweet and well behaved both at home and around town. She will forever be my heart dog after passing away at the grand old age of 14½, and not a day goes by that I don't think of her and the wonderful time we spent together. Skully, under the watchful eye of Betty, and trained by the whole family, is a dream and a delight. Obviously she still perpetrates the occasional misdemeanour (she is a bit of a barker at times, as many small dogs can be), but she is a wonderful dog who is loved by all.

Puppy parenting is about wanting to do the best for your puppy, giving yourself the tools and the knowledge to do so but still allowing for a few mistakes along the way. Now that you have made mistakes together and learned from them in the same way as I have with my dogs, I hope that your puppy becomes the happy, healthy and ever-loving dog of your dreams...And if they aren't perfect, nor are we – so be patient, kind and consistent and your life will be enriched beyond measure by simply enjoying the lifelong companionship and unconditional love they offer.

Index

Acknowledgements

Thankyou always and forever to my wonderful and tolerant wife Zo, who allowed me great dispensation as I nurtured this book into existence. The patience I write about in this book is constantly lavished upon me, as an adult human version of a puppy, by you, for which I am very grateful. Love you.

To my children, Summer, Quinn, Jackson and Riley, who have all inherited an interest in and love of animals that I am so proud of – you inspire me to continue to follow my passion for talking about all things animal.

To my incredible vet nurse and behaviourist friend Sam, who is my constant moral and behavioural guide, and helped me to update and improve upon *Puppy Parenting* mark 1.

To my supportive and wonderful family at *This Morning* and ITV, who continue to support me as I report to and help educate the nation when it comes to the health and wellbeing of all creatures great and small.

To Skully, who is a constant source of energy and light, being inherently amazing and a dream dog, who is much loved by every member of the family, both immediate and extended.

And, finally, to Betty, my first ever puppy and dearly departed Border terrier. I still love you so much and miss you every day. See you on the other side of the rainbow bridge dear friend, probably with a chewed remote control in your mouth.

Picture credits